Know Online
ADVERTISING

Know Online
ADVERTISING

All Information about online
advertising at one place

AVINASH TIWARY

PARTRIDGE

To order additional copies of this book, contact
Partridge India
000 800 10062 62
orders.india@partridgepublishing.com

www.partridgepublishing.com/india

CONTENTS

PREFACE

Digital advertising is a powerful tool that has given an immense freedom of scale and control to advertisers. It has grown rapidly in recent years and is expected to grow even more in the coming times.

Hence, understanding it is beneficial for small and big fish alike. This book is a perfect choice for both, the one who wants to enter the domain of online advertising, and the one who has tried and tested the medium but wants to master it.

As the author, I am excited while writing the preface of the book, as this brings me to the end of a journey and to the beginning of another one. Looking back, I never thought of writing a book on this topic. With so many blogs, manuals and online tools; to me mastering digital advertising looked more like self-tutored skill and that is how it came to me.

However, with my blog picking up pace, I interacted with a lot of people who expressed the need of a manual or a guide that brings together all the tricks and tips under one umbrella. I understood that creating a one shop stop to provide most of the answers for a present or potential digital marketer could mean a great opportunity. So, I put my thinking hat on and put together all the necessary lessons in this area step by step, right from basic to advanced level. That is how I recommend readers to move about- sequentially; to cover all their bases.

I must accept writing a non-fiction is a tough task. My priority was to ensure that this book has clutter free and spot on accurate solutions as I figured most of my readers would have struggled for the same online. I read a lot of articles went through multiple seminars and then at the end collated all the information in simple words for everyone understanding. Picking up things that mattered from an ocean on information was a daunting task and I remember many instances when I thought of dropping the plan of writing as it was a challenge to maintain pace with my daily routine. But the desire to spread knowledge and share my experiences pushed me through the tough times. Most importantly, my blog readers were inspirational that a small interaction with one of them would get me on my feet, working on the manuscript, again.

In the end, I feel like I have learnt so much more on my way here and I am sure the avid readers of this book will keep throwing the curveballs at me to keep me engaged and maybe for a second book on the same lines.

ACKNOWLEDGEMENT

I would like to express my gratitude to many people who saw me through this book and were with me through all ups and downs that I went through while I was on the job

A special thanks to my wife Harsha, who is a rockstar and has been my biggest support while I was dreaming and executing my life biggest challenge.

I would like to acknowledge the contribution of my sister Jyoti, who helped me so much in putting my thoughts together and without her constant poking, pushing and evoking, I could not have completed the book.

I would also like to thank my parents and parents in law, and my sister Shruti, their blessings and love made me strong to take this step forward on a new path where I was aware of nothing.

The journey was full of struggle but it became easy due to the support of my loved ones and so I thank everyone for their inputs. Where thanking family is important for their support, it is also very important for me to thank my site followers who always brought that direction to my writing and made me realize of my worth. Their feedbacks were always considered and taken serious, I really want to thank each of them, whether our interaction was direct or indirect; they have been my true motivation.

ORIGIN OF ADVERTISING

Let's look back to our past to see when advertising came into existence and how slowly the market got changed, it's really surprising to know Egyptians in 2000 years BC made use of advertising to bring awareness.

Let's go year by year to know how advertising changed over time:

2000 years BC:

At this time the Egyptians invented outdoor advertising where they advertise by etching important information in the steel in public areas.

1472:

The first print ad was created in England, it was William Caxton who printed a poster and tacked it onto church doors announcing the sale of a prayer book.

1631:

In the French newspaper *La Gazetta* the first classified advertisement was published.

1661:

First commercial ad which was about branding toothpaste Dentifice.

1776:

In the time of American Revolution, the first political ads was seen which was about encouraging people to join the army.

1835:

The appearance of the car led to the first billboard ads in the United States.

1841:

In Philadelphia the first advertisement agency was established

1873:

The first product placement in the novel "Around the World in 80 Days" by Jules Verne, in which the names of shipping and transport companies were mentioned

1882:

The first electronic advertisement was seen by replacing the billboards in New York's Times Square.

1890:

During 1890's in London *Thomas J. Barratt* became famous for his innovative advertising of soap and for this reason often referred to as the "father of modern advertising."

1892:

Direct Marketing came into existence when Sears sends out 8,000 handwritten postcards and receives back 2,000 orders.

1905:

Fatty Arbuckle, silent film star was one of the first famous people to advertise a cigarette product called Murad. The message was "Murad cigarette is the preference of men of cultivated taste".

1911:

Woodbury Soap Company uses slogan "The skin you love to touch" in the advertising world which introduced the principle of "Sex sells".

1917:

With the coming of advertisements in different form, AAAA was founded i.e. American Association of Advertising Agencies.

1920:

In his garage in the suburbs of Pittsburgh, Frank Conrad launched KDKA, the first commercial radio station in the world.

1922:

The very first radio advertisement was made

1925:

Consumerism of non-essential products was encouraged

1941:

The first official TV commercial runs for "Bulova" watches. The company took a spot of 20 seconds before the game of baseball for which they paid $9 for each spot.

Link - https://youtu.be/Ss6v5bpxODo

1950:

The first political TV ad for Gov. Dewey of New York

1957:

The birth of the longest running TV ad jingle occurs with Mr. Clean, the most famous "bald" with the longest tradition in advertising.

1970:

The first infomercial of selling homes in San Diego takes place

1978:

First spam email campaign was done by Gary Thuerk

1981:

Launched the MTV television station that advertises musicians 24 hours a day.

1984:

Apple made the most expensive commercial in the history of television advertising. It was directed by Ridley Scott, and recording costs amounted to 900 thousand dollars.

Link-https://www.youtube.com/watch?feature=player_embedded&v=G9S8J
S1qyRM

1989:

Tim Berners-Lee invents the World Wide Web while working at CERN,
the European Particle Physics Laboratory.

1993:

The first clickable ad was sold by GNN (Global Network Navigator, an
online information portal) to a Silicon Valley law firm

1994:

The website Hotwired placed its first banner ad on 27th Oct for company
"AT & T".

1994:

Started "pay per click" advertising on the site GoTo.com, which is now
owned by Yahoo.

1994:

Time-Warner launches Pathfinder with test ads from AT&T

1995:

The first keyword ad "Golf" was created by Yahoo

1995:

Pricing model CPM came into existence, Netscape and Infoseek changed
their advertising pricing model to CPM

1996:

DoubleClick was launched which gave online industry a complete new
perspective. It helped in tracking banners ads whereas also helped in tracking
ROI

1996:

First Ad Network with 30 websites was formed by DoubleClick Inc.

1996:

The introduction of Flash

1996 (End):

DoubleClick launched a product called DART (Dynamic Advertising and Reporting Targeting) which helped advertisers to track the clicks and optimize their ads before the campaign ends.

1997:

The first ad on mobile phones. Finland News Agency provided free news via SMS with advertising sponsors.

1997:

Pop-up ads by John Shiple came into existence to make advertisement more effective and unmissable

1998:

Google was founded

1999:

Search engines like AltaVista, Lycos, and Infoseek expanded their services whereas Yahoo also moved on from being just a directory of websites to a search engine

2000:

Google launches 'AdWords', which today account for 95% of total company revenues.

2001:

Pop up and Pop under ads giving 13 times more clicks then banners

2002:

Pepsi launched the most expensive advertising campaign. The commercial was for a period of 90 seconds with Britney Spears in the lead role, the total cost spent was $ 7,530,000.

2004:

Facebook launches on 4th Feb

2005:

With the birth of YouTube and began the era of video advertising and digital development of viral marketing.

2005:

Google launches its analytics platform

2005:

Ad exchange launched

2006:

Twitter got launched

2006:

Twitter's real time community provides quick and free viral marketing.

2006:

On 22nd august Facebook launches advertising

2007:

Facebook introduced the concept of behavior based advertising i.e. social behavior of users and also added opt-out feature which was not present initially

2007:

AdSense for mobile got introduced

2008:

In-Text advertising ads got popular

2008:

Facebook launched "Facebook ads for Business and also ad platform called 'Beacon'

2009:

Google launches beta test of interest based advertising on YouTube

2009:

Real time bidding (RTB) was born – a method for buying and selling display ads in real time

2010:

Viral advertising is overtakes classical models of advertising. The campaign for Old Spice got more than 30 million views and was declared the most successful ad of the year

2010:

On 13th April 2010 Twitter introduced promoted tweets and trends and the first promoted trend was Disney Toy story 3 (an animated movie)

2010:

Pinterest was launched

2011:

Online Advertising becomes No.2 in terms of budget priority for advertising worldwide

2012:

Google DoubleClick Digital marketing introduced – First modern ad platform.

2012:

First expandable ad by Pointroll

2013:

Facebook acquired Microsoft's ad platform 'Atlas'

2013:

Google launches enhanced campaigns in AdWords to target mobile devices more effectively

2014:

Pinterest starts advertising by launching promoted pins for advertisers

2014:

Year of "Programmatic Buying"

2015:

Flash ads starts to discontinue, importance of HTML5 increases

MODE OF ADVERTISING

Before we get into the world of online advertising let's have a small introduction about advertising and its division

Advertising is a form of marketing communication using different strategies to impact consumer's thoughts, feelings and actions.

Advertising can be broadly categorized into two parts:

- OFFLINE
- ONLINE

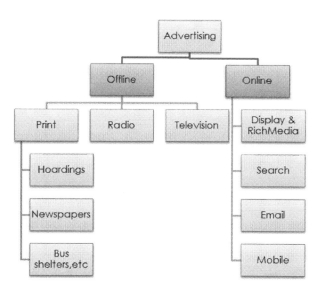

Let's know the difference between offline and online advertising which will make it easy to understand the two different world in advertising.

Both has its own pros and cons, though the technology has grown rapidly online media industry has made an important place in the last 10 years using the same.

OFFLINE ADVERTISING	ONLINE ADVERTISING
Mode of communication is physical	Mode of communication is through the internet
Approach to the customer is very slow	Approach to the customer is very fast and effortless
Success of the campaign cannot be tracked easily	Success of the campaign can be easily tracked and changes can be made accordingly
Everything here is a manual approach	New technologies being used making a lot of work automatic
Very tough to manage and requires a lot of staff	Not very easy to manage but yes comfortable than offline advertising as in online mind plays more
This still captures larger area as many don't use internet	The reach is increasing day by day but still a lot of users to cover all over
No interactivity	Interactivity here is a bigger attraction
It is tough to know much about the target audience	With rising technologies it has become easy to know your target audience behaviour well
Re-targeting is beyond the advertiser. It's all luck if the same user looks on the same Ad	Re-targeting here is much easier than offline
No source of knowing the Ads reached how many persons	In this it can be easily tracked that how many user saw the Ad
Relevant targeting is not possible	On the maximum case ads are targeted to the relevant users
People remember it very well as something physical is attached here	You see so many ads that you forget maximum of them
Location of the Ad matters a lot	Location of the ad matters here but less than as in offline

There can be many differences between online and offline advertising but they have just one similarity between them i.e. in the both the form of advertising you need to know your **target audience**!!

NOTE: Trust factor is still more with offline industry for now but day by day the trust percentage in online industry is increasing.

Let us also brief you on the subtype of advertising so that you have clear picture on different form of advertising that is quite popular:

Brief on different form of advertising

Print Advertising –

Among the all form of advertising print media is quite popular and old. There is hardly any newspaper, magazine or a magazine that can do without advertising. With the growth of online advertising, print value has slight gone down but still the existence won't get over any day as the print ad has its own target and value which is not comparable. Almost all advertisers who spend money in promotion do advertise via the print medium. Also, there are multiple advertisers whose actual target can be caught via print media only.

Print ads can be in the form of hoardings on the road or ads in newspapers or advertising on vehicles like bus, auto, etc.

TV Advertising –

One of the most effective types of advertising is advertising on television. TV ads are also considered as mass-market advertising format. In commercial breaks, brand advertises their product with a message; some big advertisers hire stars to promote their brand while smaller ones may not hire any star but any actor or actress to spread their message perfectly to a wide audience. TV advertising does not end with just commercial ads but also sponsorships and product placement within television shows. The best part of TV ads is that it allows conveying your message with sound, sight and motion.

Radio Advertising –

It's the effective means of conveying information to the audience in a very relaxed manner. The advantage of radio advertising is its mass character and availability. Radio is almost everywhere: in the subway, a café, especially while you are driving in a car and stuck in traffic, it's actually the radio that kills your time and entertains you. Still in most of the houses every morning radio listening is common over a cup of coffee or tea with family. It is all of these factors that make the advertising on the radio so popular.

Radio advertising is an effective tool in the hands of the advertiser. Firstly radio spots and audio clips allow advertisers to advertise with even the average advertising budget. Secondly, sometimes it is radio advertising allows you to convey information to the viewer as it can work where other forms of advertising (for example, outdoor advertising, BTL, advertising posters) is powerless.

Desktop/Mobile Advertising –

It's a form of display advertising which involves banners, pop-ups, or video ads on websites that you visit on internet. Mobile advertising involves showing ads on both WAP and APP. We will have a detailed study on this topic in later chapters.

Search Advertising –

One of the most convenient and effective means of advertising and promoting products and services on the Internet. It is easy-to-use, visual, and most importantly - a perfectly natural and understandable to anyone as the search ads are shown basis the keywords that you have typed on search engines. The relevancy of search ads is generally very high which makes it more popular medium than any.

Email Advertising –

A quite old form of advertising on the internet is advertising via emails. This form of advertising involves sending emails with product details via graphical representation or content, or brochure, discount details, etc. Today we can also include banner ads of multiple sizes in the emailer. This is one of the advertising which will never end as target database is known beforehand.

ABOUT ONLINE ADVERTISING

The crystal clear definition of online advertising is:

The activity of attracting public attention to a product or business through electronic media.

Looking at the word "Advertising" for 10 minutes I was trying to come out with a definition, better say the full form of advertising in context of online and ultimately I came out with a full form which defines it's meaning, i.e.

"**A D**igital form of product **V**ia **E**lectronically **R**outed **T**hrough **I**nternet **N**ationally or **G**lobally as required."

There are a number of ways you can define online advertising. It seems to look so easy but the deeper you go tougher you feel but one part always remains same is **interesting**! Advertising is always a creative, innovative, aspiring and an attractive field.

Online advertising is an advertising method through which webmasters or site owners can have their sites economically profitable and cover the costs of hosting and domain names and if the site has a greater plus richer traffic can earn in millions. It is also a way to ensure the promotion of products and services that your website offers. There are specialized companies known as" advertising firms or Ad networks" that usually are recommended to manage channel marketing campaigns. These companies are the intermediaries between advertisers (who want to launch an advertising campaign) and publishers (who are the owners of the websites accessing aside part of your ad space for the placement of advertising banners). The advertising firm receives a percentage of revenues from advertising campaigns or "costs of the firm." Usually, the costs of the firm represent between 30 and 60 percent of revenue.

Online advertising has speeded up the transactions between buyer and seller i.e. turnaround time to take an online campaign live is much lesser than the other media that we have. It also has an added feature of real-time check on the campaign performance which then helps in making the changes in between if required. Online advertising has clearly created an opportunity for advertisers to target customers accurately on their own, and help them conduct advertising in accordance with the preferences and tastes of consumers. In fact, the mass media also have the ability to target selected which is the only Internet that is capable of such targeting.

Let's get into the detail to know about online advertising perfectly.

Advantages of Online Advertising

- The first and the foremost is brand awareness
  Today online is no less than TV commercial or radio advertising and is one of the best media for brand awareness. It's a quick approach of branding about the product and making people aware before or after launching the product. Running different online campaigns help the business to spread worldwide and get hold of consumers easily. Brand awareness is very important as it helps in getting more conversion to the product, no one wants to buy unknown brands or the ones that are new to them so creating some noise about the product can save such loss

- Increase in purchase probability
  Online advertising does help in getting more conversion or business as it creates the awareness among the people about the product whereas also showing the ads to most relevant people on web making higher chance of getting the conversion for the product

- Click Through Rate (CTR)
  CTR metric can help you to know the number of people who has shown interest in your brand which is only possible in online advertising and not in offline

- Brand Perception
  It also helps in changing user thoughts about any brand e.g. any user taking Levis as a low brand or less styling trend brand may change his

perception after knowing the brand well and his ads with different designer clothes. Showing some best ads with quality features can help boost the perception of audiences. Creative plays a major role here as it's the creative which gives the first impression about the product.

- Increase in conversion rate
  As already discussed in the second point we have a higher chance of getting the business i.e. conversion. Online ads help in boosting the business as the technology and strategy used is quite advanced. The higher conversion rate can be well achieved by running retargeting placements or targeting the exact audience pool.

- High degree of affinity with commercial targets helping in reaching very specific niches which are difficult to achieve through other means. The ads are shown to the relevant person who has a greater affinity towards such products like if by his history we know the user is more affluent towards sports product we show him such ads thus making a better impact and a higher chance of conversion. Today online advertising is more about relevant targeting which is achieved by collecting audience data and then targeting them back by their interest, affinity, behaviour, etc.

- High capacity of segmentation: demographic, thematic and technological
  The technology that's being used is quite advanced now and the user can be targeted as per different segments including its behaviour, age, sex, devices, etc. The online media is more dependent on data as it's the data which helps in relevant targeting. Example: If the product is a female oriented like a dryer, the ad can be easily targeted to women only plus with age targeting of 13-45.

- Possibility of interaction and direct contact with the customer / end-user
  That's natural to happen as many customers may require more information or may show interest in bulk products, it can be any kind of interaction which may lead to an uplift of the business too.

- Limitless creative possibilities
  In online we can change the creative 'n' number of times. At times some creative doesn't work well and does not attract users, in such situations creative can be changed at any point of time with much less time and cost than offline. This change of creative due to performance issue is called **creative optimization**. Innovation in creative is very common due to uplift in technology, HTML5 has helped in adaptive or responsive creative with all possible innovation that an advertiser or agency can think.

- Constant innovation actions and format flexibility
  The best part of online advertising is that it's flexible and innovative. Every day there is some new innovation for best targeting or say to benefit the advertiser in low budget. The rise of online advertising has gone to heights due to the technical benefits that it has. No medium is as flexible and innovative as online media due to which almost all the advertiser has started to allocate maximum possible amount of budget.

- Low productions without distribution costs
  The advertiser can get their ads published with very low cost than offline media. In online you also save the distribution cost that you spend on some offline media. Online media is completely based on computer platforms and does not require any physical material to publish the ad, it just requires an initial investment to sign up with the tool and then pay for the use, basis CPM or CPC.

- Speed of implementation
  Getting the online ads live is very easy and quick, all you need to have proper knowledge of implementation and creative with you. The online ads get live instantly but for offline the implementation has some long process to work on. The process is almost real time, example: If you are using the platform like Facebook to promote, it's just a click away to take the campaign live.

Disadvantages of Online Advertising

Internet advertising has obvious advantages over traditional advertising, and also unavoidably brings its disadvantages, mainly in the following aspects:

- Insecurity
  Many consumers are still not in a hurry to make purchases through the web. In particular, they are afraid to report their credit cards even on secure websites.

- Multiple Option increases confusion
  The number of a commercial and non-commercial website is so many that consumers are neither able to meet with all trade proposals nor hold on to one site a lot of time.

- Internet speed and availability
  Today, advertisers and advertising agencies are interested in the fact that users have high-quality and high-speed internet access by which they will be able to easily demonstrate the network advertising, like television. But the true fact is that the high-speed internet is not massively available everywhere due to which consumers cannot use the opportunity to network at full capacity.

- Online fraud
  Online fraud is a common practice which creates a scare in the consumers to buy things online and that's why there are a relatively small number of actual customers online who are confident in buying things online. Though the technology has grown well and has taken multiple measures on security factor but in current scenario, there are fewer people who trust advertising on the Internet because of the rapid development of fictitious offers in the early years of this service. Though the confidence in the consumer is increasing year by year and soon the reluctance of buying online will go from the consumers.

- Visitors to their online advertising are "filtered"
  Some visitors simply do not want to see your product or is not interested in buying the same, serving impressions to them are just waste of money. The biggest difficulty lies in selecting the right online advertising target market, and otherwise, it is difficult to bring the conversion at the end.

- Lack of skills and marketing skills
  Internet advertising is the guiding ideology of the "information marketing" rather than the "impression inducement," but the expression and transmission of information still need presentation skills to attract consumers. Therefore, only the aspects of the product and the information listed here definitely do not form a successful online advertising. Traditional advertising to generate an irresistible impression and attractive presentation skills and marketing skills in online advertising is still needed, even more demanding. How to marketers to consumers in rich information resources at the same time, but also have a strong attraction for them is a huge challenge.

- Online advertising marketing personnel requirements are higher than other media:
  Compared to online advertising can almost be seen as a microcosm of the entire marketing, which involves how to attract customers to interact with customers, etc., which is the traditional advertising to customers impressed goals have to go very far. In short online advertising requires marketer's integrated use of traditional advertising performance practices, providing information on the use of soft methods of marketing and network marketing techniques.

- Your target group is outside the Internet
  Before looking to advertise online you should be sure that the product target users are available online else if your products and services have no users who are looking for it on the Internet, then the chances to attract the attention of Internet users will be close to zero. In this situation, you need to go to the usual means of advertising and marketing.

- Ad blocking technique:
The ad blocking program or ad filtering programs helps the user to block or hide the ads plus browsers today block pop-up / pop-under ads by default which then affects the reach to potential users. The blocking technique has grown faster and has been opted by many users, thereby reducing the database. If all the users start to use this feature, online advertising domain won't grow much.

Advertiser, Publisher and Ad Network

There are two sides of the industry, the advertisers, and the publishers.

The publishers are the websites which provide the content which attracts the viewers. This is the platform on which viewers will potentially view both the content and the advertisement.

The advertisers are the ones who have a product or message to market and promote to the viewing audience.

S No.	Advertiser	Publisher
1.	An advertiser is the one who pays the money to get his advertisements shown	A publisher is the one who gets money for showing the ads on his site
2.	An advertiser owns or controls the actual product or service that is being advertised because as he is the one who commands the product advertising	The publisher advertises the actual product or service and drives the user to the advertiser page to fill out the form or make a purchase or read more details on the product.
3.	Advertiser is also known as a retailer or merchant	Publisher can be an affiliate or reseller or basically a site promoting businesses
4.	Makes money by ROI, i.e. by selling the advertised product	Makes money by publishing the advertisement
5.	The ones who used Google AdWords is an advertiser always	The ones who signs up in AdSense is called as publishers where they get paid for running ads

The next image clearly shows that an advertiser is the one who buys space from publisher to show their product whereas a publisher is the one who is ready to sell its space for money; it depends on the buying type they both have agreed on i.e. CPC, CPM, CPA, etc.

The above image shows that the deal is direct between advertiser and publisher, and the buy is via networks i.e. when the advertiser buys collection of sites via ad network.

The below image shows the process of buying between advertiser and publisher.

Now, what is an Ad network?

An Ad network is a company which helps the advertiser to connect with multiple websites. The main task of an ad network is to provide the advertiser with ad spaces from multiple publishers which without the ad network is difficult to get that done manually. On real scenario, it is not possible to reach 100's or 1000's website owner to promote their product on their websites.

Ad Networks unite through a standardized process, often thousands Publisher under one roof. Similar to the marketers, they also provide ad serving, targeting and reporting. They position themselves as a cheap alternative to premium environments.

Advantage:

- Increased reach with quality
- Quick solution for mass advertising
- Easy to manage campaign on multiple websites by signing up with an ad network
- Since the Website under the umbrella has been classified category, it can serve ads to only the specified category
- Ad networks have grown up with the technology advancement and multiple targeting possibilities or automation of delivery can be done easily.
- Possible features include

Disadvantage:

- No transparency to advertiser
- Difficult to optimize the campaign due to multiple websites
- Ad relevancy is a concern at times

Types of Ad Networks:

There are two basic types of ad network:

1. Vertical Ad Network, and
2. Horizontal Ad network

S No.	VERTICAL AD NETWORK	HORIZONTAL AD NETWORK
1.	A vertical ad network is dedicated to deliver the ads to a specific audience.	A horizontal ad network is a network that delivers advertising on a wide base of inventory available.
2.	Specialized	Non – specialized
3.	Non – Generalized i.e. low global reach (general audience or targeting) but the high reach on the specific target.	Generalized – i.e. General audience (public) or targeting.

4.	Vertical ad networks offer less but exact reach for advertisers.	Horizontal ad networks offer scale, reach and numerous targeting capabilities for advertisers.
5.	It serves fewer impressions than horizontal ad network as the reach is less.	It delivers several billions of ad impressions per day as the reach is broad.
6.	It is considered as "Known buy" as you know to which audience you are targeting.	It is considered as "Blind buy" as you don't know where the impressions will serve.
7.	Some examples are Travel, Automotive, lifestyle	ROS or RON i.e. Run on sites or Run-of-network

Characteristics of Online Advertising

Compared to traditional forms of advertising, Internet advertising showing some of their own characteristics, to understand these characteristics, is to grasp the online advertising marketing strategy -based substance. On the characteristics of online advertising, and many books and articles have listed a number of surface phenomena, such as interactivity, breadth, relevance, diversity of manifestations, trade statistics, etc., online advertising does have these characteristics to a certain extent, But these basic features in this stage of practical application either not fully played out, either of these characteristics is not sufficient to explain the nature of the deep level of online advertising, it is necessary to know the characteristics of online advertising from a deeper level.

Below are the major characteristics of online advertising:

- Targeting potential customers:
  With Online advertising ads can be shown to the people who are interested in your brands and services. Also, with more targeting options available like age, demographic location, language, devices used etc. one can more precisely reach out to a specific group of people.

- Easy to track:
  Various tools like google analytics, Omniture provides us stats and data through which one can measure the performance of the campaign. We can know how many people clicked on the Ad, which Ad is performing

better, what time during the day brings maximum clicks. Considering all these results we can accordingly modify the campaign for better results.

- Budget Control:
  It's entirely up to you decide how you want to spend your money. We can set the maximum amount we want to spend on the campaign and the pattern in which it should be spent. Like during the day if the traffic is more we can set it in a way that ads shows more during the day so as to bring more clicks.

- Easy to make modifications in Ad Campaign:
  Depending on the performance of the campaign, we can easily make desired modifications so as to achieve better results. Suppose, we have an AdWords campaign wherein we see that a particular keyword is showing a better result, so we can modify other keywords on the basis of the one which is showing a better result.

- Exposure to larger group of audience:
  With more people accessing the internet, online advertising targets large number of the audience. An online ad campaign run can reach the audience worldwide. Businesses can get huge number of potential customers in the short span of time as the number of targeted audience is large.

- Specific campaign for specific audience:
  Ad campaign is designed keeping in mind the audience to be targeted. Depending on the interest of the group of user we can run specific campaigns. We have an option of customizing the campaign wherein we can select the age-group, gender, and location of the user whom we want to target.

- Software has made the process automated:
  Various software like DSP, SSP and Ad Servers has made automated process of buying and selling inventory. The bidding process has become more streamlined and transparent. Unlike traditional advertising that had the involvement of people in buying and selling process, which made it slow and less transparent.

Types of Digital Advertising

Let's start with the basic forms of Online advertising which are made using advanced multimedia technology. However, the current form of the global online advertising is primarily based on banner ads (Rich Media) which occur more frequently.

The current online advertising has the following forms of delivery:

Display Advertising:

Also known as" Banner Advertising" and is the most common way of advertising. Usually positioned to Flash, GIF, JPG and other formats on the page, but can also use Java and other languages to produce interactive, with the shockwave plug-in tools, such as enhanced expression. These are quite common forms of ad that are used by the advertiser to promote their business, there are some standard ad sizes approved by IAB, e.g. 728x90, 300x250, 160x600, etc. Some more approved sizes are mentioned under the chapter "standard sizes"

Banners ads can be static or dynamic and are image-based rather than text-based and are a popular form of website advertising.

Search Advertising:

Search advertising is a method of showing ads on those web pages which appear as a result of search query placed by the user on the search engine. Search Advertising is based on the concept of reaching out to the customer when they are looking for you. This is done by focusing on the keywords that users enter in the search engines. The keywords can be a string or a phrase. The search engine firms perform auctions to sell the ads on the basis of the bids received for keywords.

Process Used by Search Ads:

When the publisher wants to have ads served on its web page, it reaches out to the search engine firm. Search Engine relates the content of the web page with the keywords. These keywords are then placed for the auction and once this keyword gets the bid for the ads, the ads are served on the web page.

Metrics: Five ways to measure search ads: CPM, CTR, CPA, CPC, Total Time spent on the web page.

Social Media Advertising:

Social Media Advertising is the method of utilising the social media sites for reaching out to the potential customers. With million number of users daily accessing the platforms like Facebook and twitter it has become a potential place for advertisers to promote their ads. The huge benefit for advertisers is that on social sites they get large user database to target. Almost 80% of the firms use LinkedIn for hiring new employees. Social media advertising also helps in creating commercial publicity through social websites.

Advantages:

- Social websites provide the advertisers with the opportunity of attracting a larger audience as the no. of users on social websites is enormous.
- Increase in usage of mobile has resulted in social sites being accessed through mobile. So, it's easier to reach out to more no. of people.
- Social sites get an audience from a different region, people of different age group and interest. So, an advertiser can target specific audience depending on his campaign.

Email Advertising:

It is the process of reaching out to a group of people via emails. Email marketing is the most affordable, effective and targeted promotional tool. Emails may contain ads, promotional text for some brand or product, request for donation or business request. Emails cost very less as compared to other forms of advertisement like ads on TV, Newspaper ads or promotion through hoardings. No other forms of advertisement address the audience personally with their name. This feature definitely gives email advertising an edge over other forms of advertising. The performance of a campaign which is done through email advertising can be easily evaluated and traced. With email marketing audience all-around the globe can be targeted with the same level of efficiency. Sending an email to someone in the USA requires the same amount of resource as it takes to sending to someone in the UK. So, email advertising provides advertisers with greater reach. The content of the email can vary as per the requirement of the campaign. An email can contain plain text as well as graphics and animations.

Steps to be adopted for achieving better results with email advertising:

- Emails should have instructions which are easy to understand.
- Tell clients about the benefits of your product and compare it with the rivals.
- Provide client with the brief about your organisation and how business is carried out.
- Sometimes offer discounts to attract customers.

Advantages of email advertising are:

- Almost all the internet users have email ID, therefore, a larger base to advertise on.
- An email address is a broadcast push-technology, directly reaches a specific user.
- Enables personalized treatment
- Mailing lists are prepared as per interest, profile, demographic, location, etc. which you can work precisely on the target audience that you are interested in
- Sharing a promotional email or ad on email is quite easy, the recipient can forward the same to his colleague or friends
- If the email is sent to the right database, the response rate via email ad is much higher than the banner ads plus better quality transmissions to the advertiser's site

Content Advertising:

Content Ad is placed on those websites whose content is similar to that of ads. Content advertising focuses on maintaining the consistency of the matter on the site. For example: If you are reading an article on feedback on Nokia Lumia, at the end of the page you might see the article named Samsung latest phone feedback. That's a form of content advertising. Content and Native advertising is of similar form but with a slighter difference and is popularly used these days.

Video Advertising:

Video advertising is in the form of the video talking about the brand, these are beneficial as promotion can be done via sight, sound and motion.

These are generally categorised into four formats:

1. Pre-roll - The video ads that appears before the video content starts.
2. Mid-roll – The video ad appears in between the video content is running.
3. Post-roll – Just after the video content is over, the video ad starts to run.
4. Video Overlay – These are the ones that appear on the video content and can be in the form of text, banners, rich media or video also.

All these types of ads are majorly seen while playing videos in YouTube

20 Must-know terms in Online Advertising

1. Advertiser: An individual, organization or company who wants to promote its products and services with the aim of reaching out to a larger audience. The advertiser provides its ad to the publisher to show on their website.
2. Publisher: Someone who owns the website where they show the ad to promote the advertisers business. Example: Nike shoe ad on amazon. com. Here, Nike is the advertiser whose ad appears on amazon's website who is a publisher here.
3. Click: An action performed by the user/customer to attain desired information about the advertiser's product services.
4. Impression: Number of times an ad is displayed on the website. Each time the user sees the ad, irrespective of if it's clicked or not, that's counted as an impression.
5. Conversion: An action by the user which benefits the business of the advertiser can be termed as conversion. Actions like an online purchase of a product, downloading a software, sign up for services are all known as conversion.

6. Agency: Ad agency is the organization that provides services to the advertiser and advises them the best place where the ad should be displayed so as to get maximum return on investment.

7. Click through Rate (CTR): How many users that saw your ad have clicked on it too and visited your website or landing page. The Click through Rate is calculated as Clicks / Impressions. Example: Let's say your ad reached 100 impressions, and 10 users also clicked on the ad, it means your CTR is 10%.

8. Ad Network: An ad network is a collection of publisher sites for which advertising can be bought and sold on a group basis, can be big or small. Its key function is accumulating ad inventory from a contributing list of publishers and matching it with the advertiser's requirements.

9. Ad Server: The equipment that brings up the ad to potential customers is called an Ad server.

10. CPM: CPM is also called as CPT i.e. cost per thousand, which means we need to pay the cost for every 1000 impressions. It's the most commonly used measurement in advertising!! Example: If CPM is $5, it means the cost of 1000 impression is $5.

11. CPC: Just like CPM, CPC is also a measurement used in online advertising; the only difference is this cost is based on clicks and not impressions. If a user is shown the Ad and he does not click on it then there won't be any cost effect as the cost is based on clicks only. Example: If CPC is $5, it means every click costs $5 so 20 clicks then it will cost us $100.

12. CPA (Cost per acquisition): It's another word for cost per action and is used interchangeably with this term. CPA measures the advertiser's per conversion cost from start to finish, from the inclusion of the search engine results to creating interesting landing pages that grab the attention of the visitor. This means cost per acquisition measures how much it costs in advertising to convert one person from a visitor to a client for the company.

13. Ad Dimension: The size of a creative measured in pixels. E.g. 728x90; 300x250; 160x600 etc.

14. Affiliates: A type of advertising system based on the CPA payment method whereby websites run advertiser's banners for free but get paid on any sales or registrations that result from visitors that click on the banner.

15. Ad Space: The space on a Web page reserved to display advertising.

16. Banner/Creative: An online advertisement in the form of a graphic image that typically runs across the top or bottom of a Web page, in the margin, or other space reserved for ads. I.e. the Ad Space on the respective web pages.

17. Ad Tags: HTML code produced by your ad server that displays the corresponding creative.

18. Frequency Capping: A term used to describe the number of times the same advertisement is shown to the same visitor during a particular session or time frame. Frequency Capping is a popular method for ensuring that a single user does not see the same ad too often.

19. Targeting: Targeting is defined as the selection of an object of attention or attack. Same is what it means in online advertising as we target our specific users (attack) as per the requirement of the campaign. Targeting is about catching the right user at the right time at right place so that maximum output comes out of it.

20. Rich Media: Rich media banners are flash creative that employs images, text, sound, and video. They won't be necessarily interactive but are often interactive. It includes features like inviting the user to play a game, navigate through different "pages", turn the sound on/off, select an item from a drop-down, pause the video and so on. Also, another big feature that a rich media banner has is, it can use several other technologies such as Java, JavaScript, and DHTML too.

Step By Step advancement in Online Advertising

The technology has even played an important role in online advertising industry with time. Today advertising has become so exact and beneficial for both publisher and advertiser and the reason is its advancement. So let's know the stepwise advancement that online industry made to improve it from better to best!

Step By Step:

- When online advertising came into existence it was just like print advertising, it was sold based on the size of the Ad plus the price were based on expected number of unique website visitor.
- Slowly with time some more advancement came, "rotation of the Ads" in the same space of the web page got possible. (Publisher got good advantage of this as they can show multiple advertisers Ad)
- Tracking of "impressions" of a particular Ad got possible
- "Frequency capping" came into existence thereby limits on the number of impressions got possible.
- "Click through Rate" (CTR) – Advertiser started to find out how many people not only saw the Ad but actually clicked on it.
- With the time, the advertiser were started to put their expectations like number of impressions in a time span.
- "Standards" (procedures/format) started to build up for both advertiser and publisher.
- "Standard sizes" also came forward like 728×90, 468×60, 120×600 etc., which ultimately helped the advertiser a lot as they don't have to create or design new Ads for each site as publisher now had a standard Ad space too.
- "Rate models" started to come into existence like CPM, CPC, etc.
- "CPM" was the first price model in online advertising industry
- "CPC" was the next model which was used in combination with CPM, as CPC were costly.
- Due to increase in the online advertising demand, it was getting difficult for both publisher and advertiser, and this lead to the emergence of online "Ad Network".
- Flash Ads/ creatives were the next change.
- Due to betterment in the internet speed, full video nice animation, games like interactive features were introduced.
- Pop Up and pop under Ads.
- Interstitials, full page advertisements came into existence.
- Synchronized Ads.
- Demographic targeting.
- Behavioral Targeting.

- Contextual targeting
- And so on…

Today we have the best possible features in online advertising and the advancement is still on. Online industries are playing a very great job in today's world and are expected to be best among all the medium of advertising soon

Standard Ad Sizes

Why do we need any standards in sizes, I think it would be so great if we create any size of Ad that we feel like, just in case – a place of 40×40 is available on the right side of the site, we will make up the Ad of the same size and fix it up there, so great we occupied the size perfectly, but No that's not a right way!! Technically, by business perspective or by any way it won't be right way to handle things at higher level. When online advertising started there were no standardization of sizes but with time the online industries started to grow and advance a lot there was a need to make standards of everything so that everyone remains on the same page with no confusion.

With standardization of sizes, the advertiser's didn't have to design new ads for each site they advertised on, and also publishers were able to have standard designs for their pages to accommodate specific ad dimensions. The standardization helped both advertiser and publisher, the publisher don't have to worry for non-standards Ad sizes that don't fit the design of their site, just like I gave example for 40×40 ad size. And for advertiser they just have to create one set of ads and know the most sites will be able to accommodate the ad dimension they use.

I am sure you must have got the right reason for standardization so let's get to know what the standard sizes we have in online world is:

- **728 x 90:** Leader-Board
  This size is generally seen on top of the site or sometimes at the middle and bottom.

- **300 x 250:** Medium Rectangle
  Well known used size which is generally seen on every site.

- **160 x 600:** Wide Sky-Scraper
  This standard size of Ad is seen at the left or right side of the web page.

These three sizes are the most basic one used by advertiser and thus publishers are maintaining these sizes usually.

SNAPSHOT for above 3 sizes:

The IAB currently specifies number of Ad dimensions, other than above three are:

- 250 x 250 – Medium Rectangle
- 240 x 400 – Square POP-UP
- 336 x 280 – Large Rectangle
- 180 x 150 – Rectangle
- 468 x 60 - Full Banner
- 234 x 60 - Half Banner
- 88 x 31 - Micro Bar
- 120 x 90 - Button 1
- 120 x 60 - Button 2
- 125 x 125 – Square Buttons
- 120 x 240 – Vertical Banner
- 120 x 600 – Sky Scraper
- 300 x 600 – Half Page Ad

Types of Ad Categories

Depending on ad or creative, categorization of ad has been done which helps the ad server to understand what kind of ad it is picking. Categorization also helps to target the right publishers. Generally an ad other than standard or normal has been categorized, especially in the case of suggestive.

Some common ad categories are:

- Adult: Any creative or ad that has content meant for adults i.e. nudity, it should fall under adult category. Example: Condom or lingerie ads are adult categorized ads.
- Alcohol: Such category is for the ads that show or promotes any brand of alcohol. Ad having any relevance to the alcohol brand will fall under adult category. Example: Carlsberg, Blender's pride.
- Dating: Sites like Zoosk, match, or shaadi.com ads falls under this category.
- Gambling: A creative that encourages a user to gamble by purchasing a ticket, or betting money, should be classified as Gambling. Lottery and online poker are some examples. Any ad having a word "bet" also is categorized as Gambling.
- Sweepstakes: As per Wikipedia, sweepstakes are promotions targeted toward both generating enthusiasm and providing incentive reactions among customers by enticing consumers to submit free entries into drawings of chance (and not skill) that are tied to product or service awareness wherein the featured prizes are given away by sponsoring companies. Prizes can vary in value from less than one dollar to more than one million U.S. dollars and can be in the form of cash, cars, homes, electronics, etc. By this definition, any creative that encourages the user to sign up for free with the promise of a prize should be classified under this category.
- Political: Creative that promotes political parties, political views, or a candidate should be marked under Political.
- Religious: Creative that promote a religion, religious parties, or religious views, should be categorized under this category.
- Suggestive: There is a difference between the suggestive and adult categories. Not all adult ads can be categorized as suggestive or vice versa. A creative is suggestive if there is an underlying meaning to the

ad basically a double meaning ad which is not directly showing any nudity but has an adult meaning to it.

- Tobacco: Creative that promotes products with tobacco should be categorized under this category.
- Violence: Any creative that has violence, or supports violence or violent movements, should be classified under this category. Below example shows a bullet which makes it fall under violence category

Metrics and Formulas in Online Advertising

It's true mathematics never leave you and so not even in online industry it has spared you, so let's have some clear picture with examples of the formulas used in online world so that you know well how things are working in online advertising industries

CPM CALCULATION:

Cost per mile (1000) – This is one of the most used metrics on the web. It is the cost that has to be paid by an advertiser for serving 1000 impressions.

Example:
In a campaign, say an Ad of 728×90 is running and the CPM set is $5 and the impressions to be served is 2,00,000, what will be the actual cost to the advertiser?

The formula for CPM goes this way:
Cost to an Advertiser = CPM x (Impressions / 1000)

Using the above metrics:
Cost to an Advertiser= 5 x (2, 00,000/1000) = 1000
So, $ 1000 is what the advertiser has to pay!
When CPM needs to be calculated: use the final cost.

CPM = Cost to an Advertiser x 1000 / Impressions

CPC CALCUALATION:

As we know we have different rate models in online advertising, CPC – cost per click is one of the popular and well known used metric. Here the advertiser has to pay as per clicks and not on impressions. The page views can be any number, as the advertiser is concerned about clicks here.

Example:
Suppose a campaign having 300×250 size banner running at CPC of $2 and the number of clicks the Ad has got is 1000, what is the amount that the advertiser has to pay actually?

The formula for CPC goes as below:

Cost to an Advertiser: CPC x number of clicks
Using the above metrics,
Cost to an Advertiser = 2 x 1000 = 2000
So, $ 2000 is what the advertiser has to pay!

CPC = Cost to an advertiser / number of clicks

Also, Cost = Impressions * CTR * CPC.

CTR CALCULATION:

CTR is click through rate; it measures the effectiveness of any advertisement. It is calculated by using a simple formula as below:

Example: A campaign having 728×90 Ad has served 10,000 impressions and has generated 100 clicks so what will be CTR of that Ad?

CTR = (number of clicks / number of impressions) x 100
Using above metrics,
CTR = (100/10000) x 100 = 1 %
1% CTR means on every 100 impression there is one click.

CR CALCULATION:

CR is conversion rate, to calculate the conversion rate a simple formula is used:

CR = (number of conversions/Impressions) x 100,
So if number of conversion made are 20 in 1000 impressions, the conversion rate will be (20/1000)*100 = 2 %

CPA CALCULATION:

Another metric that we have and is generally used is cost per acquisition which is irrespective of impressions and clicks both. This metric deals with any action or basically when something is acquired like user sign up or when any sale is made.

Cost to an advertiser = CPA x (Impression x CTR X CR)
Suppose CPA is $5, number of impressions is 10,000, CTR is 3% and CR is 2%.
Using the above metrics,
Cost to an advertiser = 5 x (10000 x 0.03 x 0.02) = $30
Similarly, if you know the actual cost, we can easily calculate the CPA for the Ad using the below formula:
CPA = cost to an advertiser / (Impressions x CTR x CR)

Also, Average Cost Per Acquisition (CPA) = Average Cost per Click / Conversion Rate
Some more formulas that are used:
CPL / CR = CPA or
Cost per Lead divided by Conversion Rate = **Cost per Acquisition**
And,
VPA – CPA = NP or
Value per Acquisition minus Cost per Acquisition equals Net Profit.

CPV CALCULATION:

CPV is cost per visit which is new with respect to CPM, CPC and CPA but is now commonly used by companies. The costing is done as per the actual visits.

CPV = Total cost of the campaign/ Number of total visit or incremental visit after the campaign started

Suppose the total cost is $1000 and the visit increases from 50 to 250, so incremental visit is equal to 200.

Applying the above numbers in the CPV formula, we get

CPV = 1000/200 = $5

I.e. Each visit cost is $5 to the advertiser

ECPM CALCULATION: (Effective cost per mile)

Effective CPM is the actual CPM that is being applied, if the CPM set is $2 and the eCPM is $1.5, the net profit is $0.5. ECPM helps you measure how well your ads are performing. It is calculated by dividing total earnings/total spend by total number of impressions in thousands.

ECPM = (Total spent / Impressions delivered) x 1000

Example: An ad size of 728 has delivered 213456 impressions and has also spent some $300 with CPM set as $1.5, what will be the eCPM?

Using the formula,

ECPM = (300 / 213456) x 1000 = $1.40

We can also calculate eCPM using eCPC, but for that we need to know the conversion rate and then using the formula as below:

eCPM = eCPC x conversion rate x 1000

eCPC CALCULATION:

eCPC, is a metric used by Internet marketers to calculate the effectiveness of their online campaigns when the rate model used is CPC. eCPC can also be termed as "profitable per click" so if the actual CPC is $2 and the eCPC is coming as $1 per click, than $1 is the profit on each clicks.

Net profit = CPC – eCPC

eCPC = (Total spent or revenue / clicks)

Example:
If eCPC needs to be calculated for a single Ad size say 300×250, we just need to figure out how much the Ad size has spent and how much clicks it has generated, so if it is like $200 has been spent and the clicks generated are 100 with actual CPC set to $3.
Using the formula,
eCPC = (200 / 100) = $ 2
So, net profit = (3 − 2) = $1.

eCPA CALCULATION:

eCPA is effective cost per Action which is calculated same as eCPC and eCPM, It is the total spend by the total number of actions(i.e. conversions) acquired.

Example:
The total spent on the campaign is $2000 and the total number of conversions made is 200, what will be the eCPA?
Formula of eCPA,
eCPA = Total spent / number of conversions or actions
Using the above metrics,
eCPA = 2000 / 200 = $ 10

CPC vs CPM, which one to go for?

First of all, it is important to clarify each of these terms that are part of the jargon of Online Advertising means.
CPC stands for "cost per click" and reflected in the price the advertiser pays each time their ad is clicked, and this only pays for each click that effectively achieve, regardless of the number of ad impressions. As for the CPM, this means "cost per thousand", also used in traditional media, to simply put - it is the value that the advertiser pays for your ad to be seen by 1,000 people, regardless of whether they clicked or not.
In the case of Display Advertising platforms, this choice becomes important as it will certainly change the impact of the campaign, and everything must be thought according to the established objectives

Let's discuss the disadvantages and advantages of each for now. Starting with the CPC - cost per click, this has the main advantage of the fact that the advertiser only pays if the user is proved interested in the ad and clicks on it so that from the outset we only pay for the truly qualified audience. However, the disadvantage of this type of campaign leads to a higher cost for a smaller range, when compared with the CPM, since the click cost is variable and can sometimes reach values somewhat higher. Imagining that the ad is seen by 20 people and 10 of them click, the cost will be very high if we only take into account the number of people reached because of the 10 who clicked, they will almost certainly not result in 10 shopping in our online store or 10 visits to the store, but it can even happen! So it is essential to monitor in detail the outcomes of such campaigns and see if the clicks are bringing some return. In this scenario, CPM would have been beneficial.

As for the CPM - cost per thousand, these display platforms have the advantage of getting a much longer range with the same cost compared to CPC, i.e. there are many more people who (probably) saw the ad because these platforms charge for each impression and have every interest in showing the ads to the fullest. However, we may be able to show the advertisement to thousands of people being charged for it, and none of the people show interested in our ad, which is the disadvantage of the CPM against the CPC.

So if you have to choose one of these models, everything will depend on the goals you have for your brand. If it is high visibility and notoriety, it might be better CPM if on the other hand is effective and capture truly interested public the option is CPC, but should always be something thought out and integrated into other online media campaign in question.

Why Online Advertising?

There must be a thought coming once to everyone's mind that why online advertising and why not still offline or traditional advertising? Let's clear that by 10 points as below:

- It is the fastest growing medium than any other. Online advertising has grown with the growth of the internet in the world.
- High penetration on all targets, especially in the youth segment.
- Wide coverage - It comprises of targets that are highly commercial as between 17 and 55, of middle and upper class, urban habitats, with

high purchasing power, accustomed to new technologies and trends and prescribe consuming.

- Affinity - Internet is the most effective with young medium. Therefore, it is an excellent means of improving business. It is very profitable way of marketing variables (memory, notoriety, purchase intent ...).
- Targeting ability - Internet over other conventional means has the ability to reach to the desired target audience easily.
- Interactivity - By nature, the Internet allows user interaction with the goal of creating a short, medium or long term relationship.
- Creativity - The limitless creative possibilities of the medium are excellent to build an experience with the target audience. The development of new attractive formats for the user as well as video technology enables campaigns to be very effective in its objectives.
- Capacity of branding - Internet advertising improves memory and accelerates the diffusion of the advertising message.
- Feed, sale and distribution - Internet is a great medium prior to the final purchase information.
- Real time monitoring - The advertiser has the ability to obtain short-term results, since the campaign can be monitored in real time, it is easy to take decisions according to campaign performance.

I hope by now you must be having enough reason to answer that why online advertising is important and why we should invest.

Three Important Interest of Online Advertising

Profiling:

With the advent of the Internet, the amount of information has increased many times, and therefore it is possible to speak of such a thing as a web user personalization.

A user profile is created based on the observation of the behavior of the user (you click a hyperlink on a Web page, view the contents of preference, etc.), the user can provide feedback to the system (e.g. labelling web pages, content rating, which is very important in collaborative filtering).

Methods that are used to create online profiles:

- Basis on the content filtering
- Collaborative filtering
- Intelligent analysis

Now advertising on television aims to communicate massively on a brand or a product without specific profiling of the target. But in Online advertising, the diagnosis of the behavior of the user is done beforehand and that's because of the web user personalization which is done real time when the user is online. The target is selected depending on what profiling to spread its message. This precise targeting can be very effective, provided that the message is delivered subtly and that the user does not have the feeling of being "hunted".

Geolocation:

This could be part of profiling, but it deserves to be highlighted because it tends to become the sinews of war Internet advertising. The advantage of location-targeting is relatively obvious for advertisers. It is primarily aimed advertisers with an activity that is exercised only in a specific geographical area. This applies to advertisers whose campaigns are designed to create traffic in one or more specific points of sale or those who do not deliver goods or provide a service in a given geographical area. This type of targeting can be of great interest for e-marketplaces that provide deliveries in a few large cities. The geolocation may also be interested advertisers to communicate national dimension test markets or to personalize the advertising creations based on the location of the hearing.

The 'price':

Third and also very important is the price. With the same profile targeting and with specific location targeting on the Internet is significantly lower than most of the "media offline". Hence, it raises the interest of advertiser as in less spends they reaches to larger base nationally and internationally if required. Also, the multiple pricing models in online advertising makes it convenient for the advertiser to choose how does he wants to pay i.e. basis impressions (CPM), clicks(CPC), leads (CPL), engagement (CPE), etc.

Advertising Goals

Having a goal in advertising is very important, before starting any campaign the goal should be clear and the focus on it should be maintained until the end of the campaign or till the goal is achieved. There can be many goals to a campaign as it completely depends on the product and the motive of an advertiser but let's sum up them into larger points to know what kind of goals can be in advertising and how it can benefit

- Increase the visibility and awareness across the market.
- To strengthen public enterprises and commodities brand impression.
- Improve the consumer brand name purchase rate.
- To maintain and expand the market share of brand advertising.
- The dissemination of corporate and product spleen, business and information services to the public.
- To strengthen the new product promotion, popularization of new product knowledge, introduction of unique new products.
- To correct the public enterprises and brand awareness for bias, helping to remove obstacles to the sale.
- To improve the company's reputation, establishing a good corporate image.
- The promotion staff finds it difficult to reach the target market, by using advertising reaches the right target in advance.
- Encouraging consumers to shorten the decision-making process, helping in the direct purchase.
- Increase in the confidence of targeted consumers all over the world
- Through advertising, increasing the duration of use of the product plus maintaining the market rate or increase in sales of the product.
- To persuade potential customers to the sales or visit on sites thereby increasing awareness again.
- Raise awareness of the products and enhance the confidence to buy.
- In order to expand the influence of advertising, creating momentum, the morale of corporate personnel to increase enthusiasm and creative work.
- The creation of markets, and tap the potential market targets.
- To promote the development of social and cultural trends.

ABOUT MOBILE ADVERTISING

Mobile advertising – sooner or later will be a boon to online advertising and to some extent it has already been. Mobile advertising is now a rapidly growing sector providing brands, agencies and marketers the opportunity to connect with consumers beyond traditional and digital media directly on their mobile phones. With growing technology today mobile phones can be utilized for much more than just making and receiving calls like SMS, Interactive games, MMS, Photos, Audios, Videos and of course the still growing Mobile Web. Online mobile advertising has made a great use of mobile web and has made it easy for the advertisers to reach them.

The best part in mobile advertising is that the mobile phone is an extremely personal device i.e. one mobile phone typically has one unique user. This makes the mobile phone a precisely targeted communication channel, where users are highly engaged with content. As a result, the mobile channel delivers excellent campaign effectiveness and response levels compared to other media.

With going time, mobile ads are getting more interactive, today it's just not about a thin quarter-inch deep banner (static banner) which when clicked just take you to the landing page but a click on mobile banner might lead to a full screen takeover, displaying high-resolution photos or a video clip that the user can interact with or can also lead to a map, take you to a brand's Facebook page, or generate a phone call to a call centre. It's a big change in mobile advertising, too different than what we used to see some years back and due to this big change or can say the evolution of mobile rich media has made advertisers to spend and put some interest more on mobile advertising.

Mobile Advertising can be:

- Text
- Flash Movies
- Banners
- Audio
- Video

History of Mobile Advertising

Mobile advertising is predicted to become an important telecommunication's revenue and monetization strategies. Comparing to web-based advertising, there are several advantages of mobile advertising, including high penetration rate, personal communication device, individually addressable, multimedia capability, and interactive. Thus, advertisers can associate each user with fully personalized ads to increase large value of mobile ads.

Before getting deeper into mobile advertising, let's start with the step by step evolution of mobile into the market:

1973:

In 1973 Motorola was the first company to produce first portable phone, Martin Cooper, a project manager in Motorola made the first call to Dr. Joel S. Engel of Bell Labs.

1978:

Advanced Mobile Phone System, the first analog cellular system (1G network) widely deployed in North America.

1990:

The mobile phones first appeared in the market.

1991:

The second generation of mobile telecoms (2G network) was introduced in Finland by Radiolinja (now Elisa)

1992:

On December 3rd, 1992 Neil Papworth was the first person to send the world's first ever text message.

1993:

The first clickable web ad or online banner ad was sold to a Silicon Valley law firm by a website called Global Network Navigator.

1994:

Hotwired, the first commercial web magazine was the first website to sell banner ads in large quantities to a wide range of major corporate advertisers. AT&T was one of the first big companies to buy online advertising through the Hotwired site.

1994:

The first person-to-person SMS text message was sent in Finland.

1995:

Yahoo launched the first keyword ad "Golf".

1997:

Finnish news provider offered free news headlines via short message service (SMS).

2000:

Mobile Marketing Association, a global non-profit trade association representing all players in the mobile marketing value chain was founded.

2000:

The first mobile advertising conference convened in London, hosted by the Wireless Marketing Association.

2000:

Google launched Google AdWords.

2006:

Admob, a mobile advertising company founded by Omar Hamoui, now by Google launches its mobile advertising platform in 2006

2006:

Another Mobile advertising platform company, Millennial Media, founded.

2007:

Google got into the smartphone game by launching the Android phone with open-source software.

2009:

Google buys Admob for $750-million.

2010:

Apple releases its mobile advertising platform, iAd

2010:

According to eMarketer, the size of the U.S. mobile advertising market increases to $1.45-billion.

2011:

8 trillion text messages have been sent worldwide.

2011:

Mobile Services revenue exceeded $1 Trillion for the first time.

2012:

Smartphones have become one of the fastest spreading technologies in history, with 50% of U.S. mobile phone users (and 40% of the U.S. population) now owning smartphones.

2012:

Facebook launches mobile ads on the Facebook mobile app, which is used by over half of the site's 850 million users to access the site.

2013:

Total Global subscriptions exceeded to 7 billion in early 2013.

2013:

Mobile Broadband (4G) is being deployed at a faster rate than previous generations.

2014:

4G is live

2016:

5G is in process

Today's state of Mobile Advertising

It's a high speed internet generation now where mobile web is no less than Desktop web, Mobile advertising has not acquired its full goal but has created a solid foundation and has become trust able too. It's no more in its infancy stage but has stepped up to the next level. Many brands and organizations are generating tremendous results with it, showing good ROI, consumer engagement and response rates. Today almost every advertiser spends 10% - 15% of the total budget in mobile advertising and which is expected to increase more in coming days.

The trend hasn't completely changed as more than 60% people still think that mobile advertising is of no use and it brings fake clicks which is not a case today as the technology has grown faster and can catch valid or invalid clicks and same for impressions. When mobile advertising came into picture, people had concern regarding the flash creative which was quite valid as generally mobile don't support flash and running gif or jpeg won't bring any attraction to the user due to its static appearance, but as we live in a technology world we have solution to every problem. HTML5 came into existence making rich media ads possible in mobile also thereby winning the concern people or advertiser raised. And just after the involvement of rich media ads in mobile the growth started to raise more rapidly and is still in rising position, today we can do almost everything that we can do in desktop in fact more than desktop.

Top 20 Countries by Impressions: *Source: Opera

- United States
- United Kingdom
- Italy
- Canada
- India
- Indonesia
- Russia Federation
- Germany
- Mexico
- France
- Spain
- South Africa
- Australia
- Nigeria
- China
- Brazil
- Ukraine
- Japan
- Saudi Arabia
- Malaysia

Quick five points to note for an Advertiser

1. Need to have a mobile site or may be mobile optimized, great if there is a user friendly and quality mobile app. The ROI is seen to be too high as compared to the products that don't have mobile site or app
2. Please make sure to use the best technology (specially hyper-local for product based companies)
3. Have patience running the mobile banners as they take some time to show it's real worth
4. Gaming companies are playing the major role and is utilizing the best out of mobile advertising. Sooner other domains will also benefit a lot.

5. Use the best ad platform in the market and do not save money here as a good ad platform can give good analytics and detailed report which can help to analyse the campaign performance

Five major feature of Mobile Advertising

1. **Precision:**
    Mobile advertising has inherent advantages in terms of accuracy. It is a breakthrough of relying solely on traditional newspaper advertising; television advertising, online advertising and other huge coverage to reach the limitations of marketing effectiveness, but also in the audience have greatly exceeded the number of people.

2. **Immediate**:
    A phone is personal belongings, its portable nature is stronger than any other traditional media, the vast majority of users with their phones close at hand, or even 24-hour shutdown, so the user's mobile media influence is all-weather, advertising information reaches the most timely and most effective.

3. **Interactive**:
    The interactive mobile advertising is to build a platform for interaction between advertisers and consumers, so advertisers can more timely understand of customer needs, the more so enhanced consumer initiative to improve the status of autonomy.

4. **Integration**:
    The integration advantages of mobile advertising was in 3G technology development speed, mobile ads can show up in different forms of text, sound, images, animation, etc. The phone is not just a real-time voice or text communications equipment, is also a feature -rich entertainment tools: audio and video features, gaming terminals, mobile TV, etc., but also a timely financial terminals: Mobile e-wallet, securities accepted tools.

5. **Testability**:

For the owners in terms of advertising, mobile advertising relative to other media advertising prominent feature is that it can be measured or can be tracked, so that the number of accurate statistics audience.

Pros and Cons of Mobile Advertising

Mobile Advertising Pros:

Must be tired hearing mobile advertising is great or boon or is the next generation hit, etc. etc.? Let's sum up and take you with the advantages that mobile advertising has:

- Reach: Reach is maximum in mobile today. The study says mobile phone penetration is approaching 85%-90% of US population while the Internet only reach is going around 70% of homes and workplaces.
- Interactive
- Personal: Generally a mobile is not shared and is always personal so the data managed for a user by demographics, behavioral history and presence, including automatic location identification will be always correct i.e.
- Pervasive: Always with you, always on
- Measurement: As with online, it should be possible to measure the impact of campaigns directly
- Fraud resistance: Any carriers can audit usage and click-to-call can easily be verified. Fraud detection is very easy as compared to desktop advertising
- Instant results: The mobile is always carried by users with them thus the chances of looking at the ads is instant so whether the result is negative or positive is instant i.e. User response can be tracked almost instantaneously.
- Cost: Mobile advertising costs a fraction of what television and radio ads cost.
- Exact Targeting: Carriers have customer data and location information potentially available for targeting which can be very helpful
- Click Rate: It is generally high as compared to desktop advertising
- High penetration rate

- Location Targeting: Good for local advertiser and can target around their business easily
- Easy to work: It is simpler and less expensive as compared with the same for desktops or laptops advertising.

Mobile Advertising Cons/Challenges:

There's always pros and cons to everything so does mobile advertising, there are some that is being worked on and some is expected to, so as said there won't be any disadvantage of mobile advertising in coming times, but let's know the ones that are there at the present time:

- Accessibility: Small screens and limited keyboards constrain display and interactive capabilities is a bigger challenge for Mobile Advertising
- Technical: Differing screen sizes and software for mobile, other standards for mobile web and rich clients is also a big challenge while framing the ad
- Blocking: Carriers might block or impede some third party innovators
- Reach over world: The reach over world is not as high as low as consumption of mobile content is small and penetration of 3G devices is still low in most countries.
- WAP: The WAP technology is still inadequate which discourages web searching and surfing but is increasing with high pace
- Scarcity: Mobile sites as compared to desktop/laptops sites is very minimal, only 8.8% of retailers are having m-commerce site
- Data Transfer: Slow data transfer as compared to Desktop/Laptop
- User-Friendly: Mobile is not that user friendly as desktop/laptop due to its screen size; this is one of the major reasons for limiting the user using internet via mobile
- Early stage: New and still rising which will take time to create impact in the industry
- Testing Time: It takes more time to QA every ad as you need to test on both the major OS i.e. iOS and Android as they both display content differently
- Privacy Issue: It is much more than desktop/laptop in mobile so user are more concerned about it
- Not all types of ads are supported on all the devices

Discrepancies in Mobile Advertising

What is online advertising discrepancy?

It is the difference between numbers reported by a media owner/publisher and a third-party ad server which will generally differ between the publisher and the 3rd party ad server as the technology used is different at both end.

Discrepancies in mobile advertising:

Discrepancy to occur is common when you are playing with Network (Internet), we were already trying to figure it out that what is the major reason for discrepancies in Web Advertising and then we came up with the same questions in Mobile Advertising now. Discrepancy is a big problem that online advertising is going through from initial stage and is still being researched to lower the numbers as much as possible as it causes issues with reporting, billing, and of course overall performance. The more or less the reason for the discrepancy is same in mobile advertising as it was for web advertising.

Reasons for discrepancies in mobile:

- Difference in tracking method – Generally all the third party tracking is done by a pixel firing once the landing page has fully rendered while the ad serving platforms track clicks when the user clicks on the banner irrespective of the outcome of the action which will for sure create a difference in the numbers at the end.
- Cache busting – We all know that an ad can be served or reused using the cache so as to save that, a cache buster (e.g. a random number) which prevents the reuse would be implemented with the 3rd party tag to save the discrepancy.
- Time Zone difference - Different vendors may provide reports in different time zones. This is especially problematic with short campaigns and to avoid this problem it is important to make sure you're comparing these figures within the same time zone.
- Terminology – The terminology used during the approval of the campaign should be noticed so that it is same and no confusion

is formed, the metrics used may have a slight difference with the meaning for different parties which may cause inconsistency in report thus discrepancy can occur, best example: Impressions can be counted differently by the parties involved like impressions count on ad call or impression count on server call or impression count on view only, etc.

- Connection problem – As mobile device not being a fixed connection, connectivity can be an issue at times as mobile may get out of network range as the page is about to load, in this scenario ad server may register an impression but site does not.

- Third party tags – The 3rd party tags should be compatible with the publisher's SDK (software development kits), if not applicable the ad may break and may show blank impressions resulting in discrepancies.

Solution or step that can minimize discrepancy:

As this is has become a major concern IAB has started to give a deeper attention towards it and decided to form proper guidelines which when followed may lead in minimizing the discrepancy to quite some extent. They have already started this with initiatives like guidelines for MRAID, Mobile Web Measurement Guidelines, and the Mobile Phone Creative Guidelines.

Discrepancy Tolerance:

DISCREPANCY TOLERANCE

The IAB recommends a tolerance of 10% for discrepancy based on the publisher's figures.

Basic checks to reduce discrepancy:

Save Trafficking Errors:

As trafficking of tags being a manual process there is always the possibility of human error which may cause a higher discrepancy. When implementing tags watch out for some common errors including:

- Failing to copy and paste the entire 3rd party tag.
- Not implementing the correct cache buster or timestamp.
- Using incorrect 3rd party tag (JavaScript vs. I-frame in accordance with ad calls on the page).
- Difference between campaign run dates from 3rd party to publisher.

Heavy Creatives:

Please try to avoid using heavy creative (heavy rich media ads) as using heavy assets will increase the load time of Ad and website which may also result in the discrepancy. Follow the guidelines provided by IAB.

Heavy Web pages:

The way heavy creative leads to the discrepancy, similarly heavy web pages can also as ads have related effects of web page loading time. So having a less page weight will also reduce the discrepancy, keep an eye on the web page loading time also.

Testing:

Most important check that can play the main role in saving discrepancy is proper testing. A Comprehensive pre-launch testing, in conjunction with all tracking partners, to check for discrepancies before the campaign goes live will be great, also checks should be performed across a range of different mobile devices, and mobile ad formats, that represent the current mobile landscape.

Compatibility:

The compatibility of the advertiser's third party tags with the publisher/ Ad Networks or Real-time bidding platform server should always be checked beforehand.

Trusted Ad Servers:

Today there are multiple ad servers in the market who promote their platform as the best in the market but it is always advisable to go ahead with the trusted and known ad servers only.

Check the Time zone of the Reports:

As discussed earlier difference in time zone affects in data reporting which may lead to discrepancy so keep a check on the time zone of the different reports, it should always be same.

Clear communication b/w all parties:

Make sure that metrics are being defined the same by all parties involved, and therefore reporting is accurate.

Browser Issues:

One of the issues can also be browser compatibility so before making the campaign live the ads should be tested on all the version of browsers so that the ads are displayed perfectly in the live environment. E.g. JavaScript support, ad is not breaking or breaking the publisher page

Redirection of Calls:

Try to ignore number of redirections as Redirecting Ad calls can also be a cause for discrepancy as these ad calls are being called using a 302 redirect.

Reason to avoid redirections:

If there are characters inside the URL chain that the browser does not understand the URL might not be able to resolve to the correct location. The parsing code that is being used extract the data can break the chain so that no redirect can follow-through – to be able to correct this it is always a good to escape the URL so that the browser can understand characters that are not browser friendly and also the parsing code used by the 3rd or 4th party is able to process the strings correctly

There is a limitation in Internet Explorer that limits any URL to 2083 characters, by adding more and more URLS to a redirect chain may cause the URL to exceed this character limitation and there for break and redirecting will not be able to follow through. Each URL in the chain gets fired one after the other in a chain, and each URL gets parsed and then will continue on to the next URL and so on. If the user closes the browser window while this process is running, the redirecting will stop and not all parties will count.

*So try avoiding redirection of ad calls!

IMPLEMENTATION OF STUB (small program) FILE – When using an I-frame to load the ad and the ad is expandable or may run out of the frame the publisher needs to implement a stub file which will make this possible as iframe ads don't show beyond their frame. If this stub file is not implemented properly it will result in breaking of the ad and loading issue which will result in discrepancy.

Types of Rich Media Ads in Mobile

Rich Media has played such an important role in online advertising, bringing the normal banner ad from highly interactive ad, RM has also played an awesome role in Mobile advertising bringing so much of verities, today there are so many of RM ads provider like Amobee, Celtra, Phulant, etc.

Though Mobile is not much different of desktop advertising, but still has features different and with some limitations too. Let's see the different RM ads that we can have in Mobile:

- **Animation Ads:**
  This is the most common ad used in mobile advertising, generally cheap and easy to make (of course depends upon the complexity). But the richness of animation has gone so good that it looks the same as the animation feature in flash ads.

- **3 Dimension Ads (3D):**
  3D ads are special feature ads which add richness to rich media ads. In this kind of RM ad the creative rotates or tilts in with the tilting of Mobile by the user. This is a real time feature and attracts the user one time for sure.

- **Click or Tap to call Ads:**
  These RM ads have features to make a call on the number displayed on the banner as a user click on it. It is a best way to get conversion, call ads generally work awesome for search ads but still the RM also works awesome.

- **Social Bookmark Ads:**
These ads have all the social bookmarks link into the same ad, example: An eBay ad may also try to increase their users by getting the users like or join their social pages, social bookmarks includes of Facebook, LinkedIn, Instagram, Twitter, etc.

- **Swipe Ads:**
These are quite common ads for touchscreen phones having swipe feature into it, swiping may lead to next level of ad or any new image or can be used for some games too.

- **CPD Ads:**
CPD i.e. cost per download ads are ads when clicked downloads something, it can be file, software, app, etc. Depending what client want to get the download if someone clicks on an ad. Majorly these are used for InApp Ads.

- **Drag Ads:**
Another RM ad with a fascinating feature of dragging on the ad, you can drag and drop on the creative making it go to the landing page after successful drag and drop

- **Dynamic Location Overlay banner:**
These RM ads show the distance of the shop from the user, it is dynamic as the user changes its place the distance changes accordingly on the banner. Example: Mc Donald ad showing distance with the banner ad, so any user who is around the shop will be shown the advert with the distance on it making the higher chance of conversion.

- **Shake Ads:**
As the name says these kinds of ads has the feature of shaking, with the shaking of the mobile there can be many features added like a change of color, change of image, opening of the video, or opening of the main advert etc.

- **Map Ads:**
  Ads having map into it is a very useful feature and thus having a good success rate for the advertiser having physical shops, these kinds of ads contain a map which shows the route to the advertiser from the current location which is an additional and a useful feature for the users seeing the ad.

- **Camera Ads or Instagram Ads:**
  These rich media ads have the feature of taking a live picture and then sharing it. It's a playful feature which attracts users this giving a good notice to the adverts. The ad asks for an image into it where you can take your own image and integrate into it which later can also be shared as the ad contains the social bookmarking feature too.

- **Twitter Feeds Ads:**
  These ads are different of social bookmark ads as in social bookmark ads it has only the link button on the ad but in twitter feeds ads show up some previous tweets made for the advertiser, it can be the stored one or can also show the live, depending upon the requirement of the client that they want to show the favourite ones or all the live tweets.

- **Wipe Ads:**
  A great feature for touchscreens phone ads, wipe ads are first shown with some moisture over an image or snowy ad which when wiped shows up with the actual content.

- **Paint Ads:**
  Another playful feature attracting users and thus higher user engagements is having painting feature into the ad. These ads contain features of adding your own painting or by quick painting on the ad.

- **Gaming Ads:**
  Gaming ads are ones having the attractive game on it making the user play and thus with successful completing may ask for email id, name or any information. The ads may be a puzzle, shake related ads, etc. These ads are famous for higher engagements.

What is MRAID?

Definition:

MRAID stands for "Mobile Rich Media Ad Interface Definitions" is the IAB project for mobile rich media advertising to define a common API specification. The standardization helps to keep everything at one level thereby keeping the creative creation smooth. In clear words, MRAID suggests the common commands that every creative developer follows while making the creative whereas the apps who support MRAID also follows the same command mentioned in the MRAID which in result makes a perfect synchronization of creative and apps. As a result, the same creative can run across different applications from different publishers.

The universal guidelines in MRAID solve the interoperability issues between publisher mobile applications, ad servers, and different rich media platforms. These guidelines provided are regarding the ad interactions and actions like:

- Expand
- Collapse
- Resize
- Close
- Additional Functionalities within Ad
- Screen size
- Video play
- Save picture on your device
- , etc.

NOTE: MRAID is required only in case of creative running on APPS and not on Mobile WEB!

MRAID version:

Currently there are two versions-

1. MRAID V1 (1.0)
2. MRAID v2 (2.0)

MRAID v1 supports rich media advertising core component which includes very minimal requirement like displaying HTML ads, expand or collapse to a fixed size within a container whereas MRAID v2 adds support resizable creativity, and provide more control then what MRAID V1 provides. The ad designer gets more functionality or control over rich media ads like which ultimately gives an ease to create more functional banners.

NOTE: MRAID V2 incorporates the functionality of MRAID v1 so the SDK compatible with MRAID v2 can easily support MRAID v1.

Six key goals that MRAID shows importance to:

- High Interoperability - An ad which supports MRAID should be feasible to run on any platform or app compliant of MRAID
- Flexibility - Publishers (SDK) are given the flexibility of allowing or disallowing the MRAID features for an ad
- Close Button - MRAID compliant ad should always have an exit button i.e. when the user wants to come out of the rich media ad experience can come out anytime.
- Graceful Degradation - MRAID compliant ad has the ability to degrade the functionality when required. The purpose of graceful degradation is to prevent terrible failure.
- Progressive Complexity - The MRAID compliant ad should not be too complex but simple in its functionality. The features should be added in stages to know the effect on the creative execution of different apps.
- Consistency in communication between ad and app - One of the important goals of MRAID is to provide consistency between rich media SDK's and ads so as ads can easily communicate with SDK's regarding expand, collapse, or open app's embedded browser

Implementation:

MRAID script needs to be added before any of the MRAID function is called, generally adding it to the <head> is recommended. Once the MRAID script is invoked by the debugger all the MRAID libraries are injected, after which any function relating to MRAID functionality can be called.

MRAID Script:

```
<script src="mraid.js"></script>
```

Recommended in the start of the code as below:

```
<!-- use script tag to identify this creative as MRAID -->
<script type="text/javascript" src="mraid.js" onerror="console.
log('mraid.js not found');"></script>
```

Why MRAID?

To understand why we use MRAID first let's know about the two type of ad creative that run in mobile platform:

1. Mobile web creative
2. Mobile InApp creative

Mobile web creative – These creative are same as web creative that run on web browsers. These creative run within an iframe (container) which can easily communicate with the container via browser as both works on the same language i.e. HTML5/JavaScript. The creative can ask the browser to perform the action like expand on the iframe and this can be done is nanoseconds (completely depends on the creative size)

Mobile InApp creative – These creative are the one which run within apps and not browsers and the apps are not running on HTML5/Jscript thus the communication between the creative and container does not happen. These apps run on their native code of the devices i.e. Objective-C for iOS or Java for Android.

Above is the place where MRAID comes into action as it defines set of instruction that allow creative to interact using JS with objective-C/Java. As creative can interact only in HTML or Java and apps can understand only their native language i.e. Java in case of android and Objective-C in case of iOS there is a need of intermediate which can help smooth interaction. Thus, this need is fulfilled by MRAID which helps in smooth conversation between InApp creative and apps in which the ad is running.

Therefore using MRAID can make the rich media ads run on the application using MRAID compliant SDK's plus enabling the creative agencies and rich media developers/providers quickly create rich media creative that can run on different apps and thus don't have to create multiple creative for different apps.

MRAID Testing:

Once you have both the MRAID compliant creative and MRAID compliant SDK, the step that you need to take is test some sample ads to confirm the complete compatibility are:

- Single-Part Expandable Ad
- Two-Part Expandable Ad
- Full-Page Ad
- Resize Ad
- Resize Ad Designed to Cause MRAID Errors
- Video Interstitial Ad

We have a free tool available by IAB to test MRAID compliant ads which is very easy and makes your life smooth during testing phase. http://webtester.mraid.org/

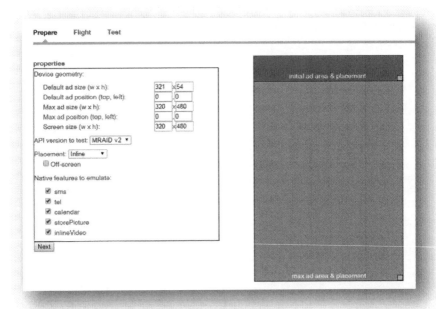

MRAID three major Advantages:

1. Multiple Platforms – MRAID provides common platform or API (application programming interface) which helps in smooth communication between the creative and apps and if the creative and API both is MRAID compliant it can easily run on any apps without any concern
2. Time Saving – Following MRAID saves a lot of time in creative building as it does not require to creative different creative for different apps
3. Cost efficient – With time this also helps in cost saving, as multiple creative creation cost more than creating the creative once

Why MRAID is important?

- Time spend on apps - Today major time on mobile is spent on apps than mobile WAP/web, so to target maximum reach we can't ignore advertising on apps.
- Time Saving – As already mentioned above that following MRAID saves a lot of time because then the developers don't have to create multiple banners but just one which can run across different apps
- Standardization – Standardization makes life easy as everyone follows same set of rules thus saves a lot of confusion as no one creates in their own understanding
- Multiple/Customized rich media banner – Very importantly using MRAID can help advertiser run multiple types of rich media banners with own choice of customization in it.
- Cost saving – Cost is always an important factor which can be saved a lot by using MRAID compliant ads.

Difference between VAST and MRAID:

S No.	VAST	MRAID
1.	VAST full form is "Video Ad Serving Template"	MRAID full form is "Mobile Rich Media Ad Interface Definitions"

2.	VAST is used as a standard for video player	MRAID is used as a standard for mobile rich media (video) advertising
3.	This standard defines the communication between the video player and the ad server which basically controls the placement of video advertising	The IAB MRAID standard allows rich media advertising materials together using standard technology to deliver the apps without having to integrate advertising in the platform-specific programming of the app.
4.	VAST also ensures that video advertising can also be linked via a redirect	MRAID ensures to run almost all kind of rich media ads on mobile apps
5.	VAST is a script for the video ad which gives consistent instructions to the video player on how to handle an ad	For the creation of Ads MRAID provides only HTML5 and JavaScript.

NATIVE ADVERTISING

Definition:

Native Advertising was first proposed by Fred Wilson saying it is not a form of advertising but a marketing concept. In short, native ad is "a special kind of media forms designed to allow advertising to become part of the content." It is an ad on a website or platform while maintaining the format and editorial style of the rest of the information on the site, to conclude on definition it is not the traditional display advertising formats, but integrated online ads on pages using the contents as an advertising medium.

Forms:

Native advertising can be a video, pictures, articles, music, or other forms of media. The "content marketing" is also a native of another form of advertising, Often you see at the end of the article saying "Other articles you might be interested in," in which some of which may be the companies paid by. Native advertising does not refer specifically a particular form of advertising, but an advertising concept. According to their media properties, flexibility finds a balance between media features, user experience and advertiser effectiveness and is a win-win situation for all.

Latest trend but old concept!

It's the latest trend in advertising and is being quite liked my many advertisers and consumers too, the concept is quite simple by providing content of interest to users of a medium or information platform so that the content is consistent with content and user experience of that environment or platform. In simple words, providing branding content around the website relevant content which is likely to be read by users as of same interest and thereby giving more exposure thus indirectly advertising the product or brand. But to the actual fact, the native advertising is not something completely new. The concept of sponsored content has been managed for decades in TV, magazines, newspapers and radio; but now it's famous online and catching the interest of advertisers.

This is working great as it doesn't look like some external ad on the website which many users on the site ignore having a feel of external or looking it at as a promotional stuff, but with native ads the feel is different as it's not an ad but recommended content giving more insight about the relevant product.

An important aspect of Native advertising is that to be effective it must be consistent with the format and user experience. Having said that the content and format should be similar to expect from editorial content, it is important that the native advertising should be clearly identified as such (typically by a legend of "Featured Content"). On one hand, this has to do with caring ethics and credibility of the media in question, but the other side can even help increase advertising effectiveness. Yes, the native advertising (when properly executed) causes the following effect: When a user goes to a website that likes / respects and sees that a brand is providing valuable and interesting to the site content, and supporting it financially so that I can survive, this creates a positive perception in the user toward that mark.

There are two types of Native Advertising such as Indoor and Outdoor:

1. Indoor:
   This applies to brands that create content or profiles within existing platforms (for e.g. Twitter, Facebook, YouTube, Pinterest) and then promote the content using the same look and feel of the platform on which it is located.
   It should be noted that this is all working manually within the possibilities offered by the platform.

2. Outdoor:
This content is created by the brand outside of any existing framework. The content is then distributed through third party services (company) on different platforms. These third-party services adapt content to different styles and formats, depending on the platform on which the content will be published.

There are many different companies that offer this kind of service and most other than the publication of content on different platforms also offers a publication on the different types of devices in a variety of formats. Open type of Native Advertising-offers the level of automation that you do not have at closed.

Classification:

Native Ads are classified into six formats as per IAB, let us know them all -

- In-Feed Type:
It is the ad that displays between the content of the websites or application. It get synchronized with the content and does not appear like an ad. In recent years, text or banners ad is no more uncommon which will attract much of user's attention thus we can expect in-feed advertising to do wonders in the digital business media

- Paid Search:
In other words it can be called as listing advertising as it appears in the similar format as the search result of any query.

- Recommendation Widget Type:
This type of native ad is done via widgets or recommendation column on the website. While reading an article you may see "recommended articles" or "You might like" under which promoted content or article link will be shown where clicking on it will take you to the detail page. The advertisement (native ad) to be displayed to the user is customized and is shown as per targeting the required people.
Since it is often displayed at the bottom of the page, visibility is often lower than other ad formats.
*The listing could be in a form of images also.

- Promote listing type:
  It is the advertisement that is displayed in a similar format as the actual search results and is generally seen at the top of search results matching the word that the user searched.

- In-Ad (IAB Standard) with Native Element Units:
  This type of ad is same like display ad but with an exception of having content within it. The ad fits within the standard IAB container outside of the editorial well but is contextually relevant to the content around it.

- Custom Type:
  This type of ad is the one which does not fall under any above five types. E.g. Native ads on Pandora

Features:

- Value of the contents: Native advertising is valuable for the audience to provide meaningful content, rather than simply advertising information, but this information can provide users meet their lifestyle, lifestyle information.
- The original nature of content: The content and presentation of the implant does not destroy the harmony of the page itself, rather than to grab the attention of consumers and unexpected presents, destroy the harmony of the picture.
- The user's initiative: User willing to read, willing to share, willing to participate. Rather than simply "to me so far," the advertising communication, but each user can become interactive sharing formula diffusion point spread.
- Visual integration: The ad building in user experience among
- User-driven: advertising does not interrupt the user experience, no interference;
- Content is king: Brand to push the real value to user's content.

Importance:

The true fact is everyone is running out of time and is in search of quick answers to anything, so when a user is searching something online any related information grabs the interest of user else wise everything is ignored. The fact is with the development of society, the consumers have become smart and believe in their own finding of the brand or product before making a final call, and they tend to find relevant information on their own using different channels where online being an easy platform now. Thus making use of native ads a great success as it looks like an internally related stuff to the user giving positive remark to the reader.

Difference between Native Advertising and Content Marketing/Advertising:

S.No.	Native Advertising	Content Marketing
1.	Ad Format – Look and feel of third party website	Ad Format – Same format as companies own website as posted in the same domain
2.	Hosted – Content is hosted on third party website or platforms like Facebook, buzzfeed, etc.	Hosted – Content is hosted on brand's own website or blog.
3.	Involvement – Third party involvement is necessary	Involvement – No third party involvement is there as everything is self-managed and hosted at own domain
4.	Look and feel – Sponsored posts which can be in a form of text, image, video	Look and feel – Mainly text with images, videos or charts
5.	Costing – Content creation and ad space costing is involved	Costing – No ad space costing as no third party involvement is there

Examples of Native ads are:

- Sponsored videos: The video recommendations in search results. Platforms – YouTube, Vice
- Sponsored Playlists: Playlists cover photos can be linked to URL's, playlists can be created by companies. Platforms – Spotify, iTunes

- Sponsored posts: Posts produced by companies blend into original content. Platforms – Facebook, Twitter
- Sponsored Stories: Stories produced by companies mix with other content. Platforms – Mashable, Atlantic
- Sponsored Listings: Advertised listings are shown in search results. Platforms – Amazon, eBay
- Sponsored links: Promoted links appear within search results. Platforms – Google, Bing

Native Advertising Challenges:

- Ad Standards - No set standards or performance benchmarks yet exist for most forms of this new advertising category
- Product Efficiency -Unlike display ads, native advertising often requires creative management to tailor content to best serve the user
- User Trust - Publishers can maintain user trust by creating content that adds value and by refraining from disgusting ads
- Brand Integrity - Presenting brand integrity may mean turning down easy money gained in the short term through brand partnerships
- Clear identification of the content - Despite the fact that a paid contribution is included in the layout of a publisher, they must take out clear place labelling of Native Ads, e.g. 'Sponsored'.

Reason for the success of Native Advertising:

- Major use of ad blockers in the browser
- Downfall of CTR with time - Fact is 99.8% of banner ads are ignored and the pre-roll skip rates are rapidly increasing
- Much liked concept by Advertisers
- Performance - No benchmark has been yet finalized but the performance is far better than the normal display ads
- Relevancy - Display ads shown on some website has no relevancy to the page but with native it's always relevant which is of great interest and likeliness by the users too.
- User's experience - Far positive then display banners, people show interest interacting with native ads

- Native Ads can be displayed easily on small mobile screens, which further increases their relevance

Advantages:

- Advertising Effectiveness: Overall, the attitude towards native content or ad is mostly positive. One big reason is that the maximum ads are relevant and are well blended in the content around.
- Mobile: Native ads format are well suited for mobile devices and are also seen that the native ads on mobile perform better than the desktop. But the growth of native ads and awareness of advertiser towards the same is important and should increase.
- Additional revenue for publishers: By incorporating native advertising formats publishers could generate additional revenue. The good part of native ads is they don't occupy additional space on the website and are generally incorporated in the content place.

Disadvantage:

As such native advertising does not have major disadvantages except some below ones:

- Cost Intensive
- Time Consuming
- Ad Blockers may start blocking the same
- Customer once gets used to the concept, may start ignoring and as it's a time consuming and costly may lead to a failure soon

RICH MEDIA

Definition:

The advertisements with which users can interact in a web-page format are rich media's. They may appear in ad formats such as banners and buttons, as well as transitional (interstitials) and various over the- page units such as floating ads, page takeovers, and tear-backs.

Rich Media refers to the utilization of various technologies to enhance a recipient's experience. It uses advanced technology such as streaming video, flash, HTML5 to interact instantly with the user, also the term of rich media is not easy to define, but all the rich media technologies generally exhibit at least some of the following characteristics:

- Allow for advanced animations,
- Support audio/radio in the advertisings,
- Instant user interactions, etc.

The defining characteristic of rich media is that the media element exhibits dynamic motion and this motion can occur over time or in response to an interaction with the user too.

To define in simple words, Rich media banners are interactive creative that employs images, text, sound, and video. It includes features like inviting the user to play a game, navigate through different "pages", turn the sound on/off, select an item from a drop-down, pause the video and so on. Also, another big feature that a rich media banner has is, it can use several other technologies such as Java, JavaScript, and DHTML too.

Features of Rich Media:

- Highly interactive i.e. it exhibits dynamic motion
- It includes audio and video
- Higher-quality content
- It can also include flash games in the banner that can be played by the user
- The size of the file is generally heavy; the size depends on the creativity it holds
- Technically advanced and engaging
- It's capabilities make advertising even more useful, letting a viewer interact with an ad and learn about a brand without having to leave the page they're on

Rich Media in Digital Advertising:

Rich media in digital advertising is a boon to digital marketers or say, advertisers, all the advertisers make use of rich media for introducing their brand, products, services or special offers with video, audio and some user interaction as it brings more attention of users towards the Ad. The rich media technology plays a smarter role here leaving a much better impact on users than banner ads.

There are many pros and cons that rich media has but the main advantages of rich media over standard banners are:

- Impact – Due to its richness and highly interactivity rich media leaves a greater impact on users, rich media ads are generally more engaging and thus chances of getting a conversion is more.
- Visibility – Visibility of the ad on a page becomes more due to its interactivity and thus it is properly visible on a web page and thus grabs the attraction of a user, plus visibility increase more as the message can be shown in divide way (step by step)
- Higher Conversion rate (CR) – Rich media ads have generally higher conversion rate due to its attraction towards the users
- Higher Action Rate – Action rate is the percentage of interactions that incurred an additional activity. It is always higher in case of rich media

- Higher Interaction Rate – It is the percentage of users who interacted with ad unit in some way
- External Features – With rich media we can do almost all kind of tracking, like engagements, time duration, survey addition, etc. we can track all the activity done by the user on the ad. We can also add external elements like a map, video from other server, twitter feeds, etc.
- Social Bookmarks – Social networking is also a great way to promote, rich media ads are also handy for this feature, we can add social sharing like Facebook, LinkedIn, pin interest and can also add other features like showing of live twitter feeds using XML.
- Reporting – To know the success rate of the ad or campaign we do need data, and rich media is rich in providing all kind of data too
- Interactivity – Highly interactive
- Works with almost every ad server
- Fast, painless modifications, even on live ads
- Video Integration is possible into creative concepts.

Common Rich Media Metrics in Mobile Advertising:

- Dwell rate - The percentage of users exposed to a given piece of rich media content or advertising who interact with that content moving their cursors over it (but not clicking).
- Interaction rate - The percentage of the audience that engages with the ad unit.
- Interaction time - Amount of time users spend engaging with the ad.
- Display time - How long on average the ads were displayed on the web page.
- Expansion rate - This metric is used for expandable ads, the ad expansion rate is the ratio of ad expansions to the number of ad impressions.
- Video views and completions - The start and finish rate for video ads, starts and completions data can provide important information on levels of user interest
- Average video view time - Another way to gauge the popularity of video ads with viewers is to compare the average length of play with the total length of the ad

- Video pauses, rewinds, mutes - some rich media tracking systems also enable advertisers to track actions like pause, replay, mute, etc.
- Close - Close event is also tracked as it helps in calculating the expansion or dwell rate
- Custom events – Internal tracking, mouse over, downloads, etc.

Common Rich Media Types:

TYPE	ABOUT/DESCRIPTION
EXPANDABLE	These are the ones which expand when a user moves his mouse over the ad or clicks to interact with it, they also come in pre-expandable format i.e. when the page loads the ads are seen in expanded form
IN-PAGE	A rich media ad that has functionality within the same ad (file, it does not expand or anything), like games, animation, video, forms or brochures. In-stream medias are part in In page units
FLOATING	The ads that appear as a layer on the top of web page, these are called floating ads as they float above the web page and do not have any base ad like collapsed unit of expandable banner
TRANSITIONAL /INTERSTITIAL	These ads play in the main browser window between two pages of a website. When a user clicks on a link, they are taken to the advertising page, instead of the page they requested. They usually have small file size and are not pre-cached
TAKEOVER	The ads that replace all or part of a publisher's web page with advertising content, they are often designed to look as if they are breaking or otherwise interacting with web page content
POP-UPS	Ads that launch a new smaller browser window that appears above the open page, it launches automatically on page load

Difference between
Standard Banner and Rich Media:

S No.	STANDARD BANNER	RICH MEDIA
1.	Standard banners are simple banners of gif, jpeg or flash. They usually include text with a visual such as a logo or a graphic	Rich media are those ads which has audio/video in it, i.e. rich with its behavior
2.	Less in size, advantageous when the purpose is only branding	Heavy file size
3.	Less or almost no interactivity i.e. STATIC	Highly interactive i.e. DYNAMIC
4.	No other technology can be used with standard banners	Rich media can synchronize with technologies like Java, JavaScript, DHTML also
5.	These only have one interaction i.e. on clicking it leads to advertiser landing page	It can have number of interactions

AD SERVER

Definition:

The equipment that brings up the ad to potential customers is called an Ad server.

The first central ad server was released by FocaLink Media Services and introduced on July 17, 1995.

An ad server is a computer server, specifically a web server that stores advertisements used in online marketing and delivers them to website visitors or users. The content of the web server is constantly updated so that the website or web page on which the Ads are to be displayed contains new advertisements every time (when the site or page is visited or refreshed by a user). The one of the purposes of ad serving is to deliver targeted ads that match the website visitor's interest.

As part of the ad operations process, ad serving is the main procedure. Ad serving serves the function of allowing the ads to appear on the website from the ad server or web server. The ad server is responsible for delivering content such as banner advertisements, banners consists of static images, such as, jpg or gif and rich media; flash files and expandable JavaScript tags that allow for more animated media. Ad serving tracks the impressions and clicks that the ad campaign delivers, it allows a measure of how the campaign is doing for the client.

Ad Serving Techniques:

Ad servers bring a new innovation in how publishers can measure their website traffic and the functionality of them is growing in providing techniques that allow the publisher to be more marketable to their clients' needs. There are several types of ad server techniques like ad targeting, behavioural targeting, and ad metrics.

- Ad Targeting: ad targeting can simply be defined as the narrowing of a certain class of the population
- Behavioral targeting: Behavioral targeting occurs after the target market of the ad is determined. It is defined as specifying ads to different links that have a similar interest that a user visits frequently.
- Ad Metrics: Ad metrics notifies ad traffickers when the stats for ad views are low and prompts them to discuss new ways of reaching the company's target market for the product being advertised.

Types of Ad Servers:

- Remote Server: Servers run by the third party which helps in serving the Ads across domains owned by multiple publishers. They deliver the ads from one central source so that advertisers and publishers can track the distribution of their online advertisements, and have one location for controlling the rotation and distribution of their advertisements across the web.
- Local Server: Local ad servers are typically run by a single publisher and serve ads to that publisher's domains, allowing fine-grained creative, formatting, and content control by that publisher.

Features of an Ad Server – How does it help?

- Track the number of impressions delivered by each campaign
- Track the number of clicks delivered by each campaign
- Ad server helps publishers to monitor and manage the available ad space on a website
- Targeting ads to different users, or content
- Help in optimizing the campaign in an easy and better way
- Serving multiple ads quickly and to targeted users
- Frequency capping – A term used to describe the number of times the same advertisement is shown to the same visitor during a particular

session or time frame. Frequency Capping is a popular method for ensuring that a single user does not see the same ad too often.

- Geo-targeting
- Behavioral targeting
- Time and day parting
- Action tracking – Most ad servers track post-click actions, such as leads, sales etc. that happen after a user clicks on an ad and goes to the advertiser's site. Etc.

Note: With coming advancement ad server features are increasing day by day.

First Central Ad Server

The first central ad server having Pentium 66 processor was named MANGO (image below). Focalink re-launched the ad server under the name SmartBanner in February 1996.

The first local ad server was released by NetGravity in January 1996 for delivering online advertising at major publishing sites such as Yahoo and Pathfinder. NetGravity, founded in September 1995 by Tom Shields and John Danner based in San Mateo, Calif., is the proven leader in online advertising management software. In 1998, the company went public on NASDAQ (NETG) and was purchased by DoubleClick in 1999. NetGravity Ad Server was then renamed to DART Enterprise.

General Working of an Ad Server:

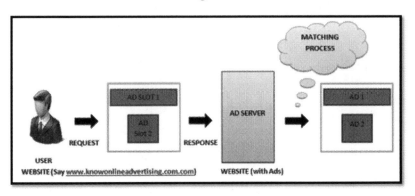

Steps

- User visits to a website, say yahoo.com where yahoo has two ad slots on his homepage.
- Website is loaded with its content (retrieved from its web server), similarly, the ad slots on the page try to retrieve the ads
- The request is sent to the ad server for the ads
- Ad server performs number of steps internally before sending an ad; ad server goes for a matching process, some matching process includes:

  1. Frequency capping
  2. Running optimization algorithms, to check the performance of an ad
  3. Advertiser parameters, including a site list, time of day, geography, browser type, etc.
  4. Publisher conditions(Ad blocking)
  5. User data, which is information about a consumer's past web behaviors or demographic collected by the advertiser, a data company, or the publisher, etc.

*These matching and checking are done in Nanoseconds

- After matching process, ad server responses with the most appropriate ad to be served on the website(yahoo.com)
- User views the content on website with ads on their respective slots

Functionalities of an Ad Server:

- Track the number of impressions and clicks delivered by each campaign.
- Targeting ads to different users, or content.
- Prevent campaigns from appearing on pages with semantically controversial content.
- Geographic and Behavioral targeting.
- Optimization and tuning for better results.
- Frequency capping (how many times an Ad should appear to a single user)

Detailed Operation of an Ad Server:

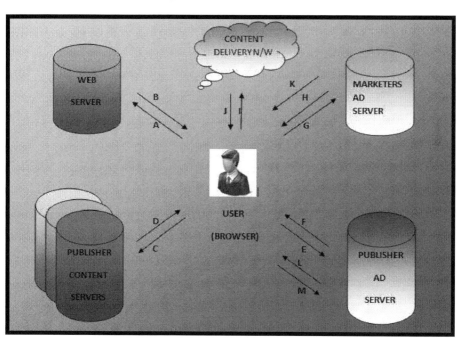

Pictorial representation of rendering of an AD

STEPS:

(A) - When a browser navigates to a publisher website, (B) the publisher's web server sends back a bunch of HTML code.

(C) - The HTML code tells the browser from where to get the content i.e. from which content server. It also tells the format of the content on the page. (D), the content server returns the content on the page or browser.

The part of the HTML code returned to the browser also includes a coded link known as an ad tag.(E), the link redirects to the publisher Ad Server which (F) returns an Ad to the browser.

There are times when the publisher Ad server sends back another ad tag (link) which redirects to a marketer Ad server from where the Ad has to be fetched. These redirects are temporary redirects, technically 302 redirects.

(G) - The browser now calls the Marketer's Ad Server which itself (H) returns with a link to content delivery network i.e. CDN which is a global network of cloud servers that actually house the raw creative graphics to fetch the actual ad.

(I) - The browser redirects to the CDN, (J) which returns the creative or Ad to the browser and the relative Ad is shown to the user.

(K) - One more important step that occurs when the Market Ad server returns the CDN link is that it also send the redirect link of a 1x1 image.

(L) - When the browser fires this last redirect calling a 1×1 pixel from the Marketer's Ad Server, (M) 1x1 fires.

NOTE: *Once the publisher's ad server sends the browser a redirect to the marketer, it counts a delivered impression in its own database.

*When the browser fires this last redirect calling a 1×1 pixel from the Marketer's Ad Server, the Ad Server knows the ad was successfully downloaded and it finally counts an impression in its own database also.

*Clicks are tracked in much the same way as impressions, with redirects.

Difference between an
Ad Server and an Ad Network:

S No.	AD SERVER	AD NETWORK
1.	The equipment that brings up the ad to potential customers is called an Ad server	Ad network is a company that connects advertisers to websites that want to host advertisements
2.	In simple words, Ad server is a tool used by ad agencies and/or clients to facilitate ad trafficking and to provide reporting on ad performance	Ad networks are a single buying opportunity for media buyers and an opportunity to access advertising market for small publishers
3.	Ad server is a part of an ad network	Every ad network has their own ad server
4.	There are two main types of ad server – Local ad server and remote ad server	There are mainly three different types of ad networks - vertical, horizontal, and targeted networks
5.	The ad servers provide data like impression served, the number of clicks, CTR, leads, etc.	The ad network provides data to client retrieved from an ad server (every campaign has its own data)
6.	The use of the best ad server provides consistent and maximized feature like action tracking (post-click activities) such as sales, leads, downloads, engagements, video tracking, etc.	The use of a best ad network allows an advertiser to assure that their ads are placed on the best possible website to target their ads towards their target market

What are the reasons for discrepancies on an ad count between the third party and own ad server?

There is never a sure shot reason for such discrepancies but yes we have possible reasons out of which one or may be more than one be the cause of the discrepancy. Let's know the possible reasons below:

- Counting mechanism of the ad servers:
  Very important reason to look after, is the mechanism that two different server follows, generally, all the ad server has the same

algorithm especially the basic of counting but it may differ with the hyper-technology and customization. Just the way, Hyundai and Ford basics may be same but the feature may differ with the high standard technology

- Wrong set up:
  Common reason for the discrepancy could be the issue in campaign setup. The issue could be on any of the ad servers so both sides is checked step by step to see if anything is not missed. A lot of time tags are missed with cache buster macro which increases the difference in number between two servers.

- Broken tags:
  A tag is a JavaScript or HTML code where a small mistake within the code breaks the tag. There may be scenario at times when the tag works on the local system but once it goes live, the tag does not work. The tag should be checked properly, and is always recommended to not change anything in the code as a system generated has a proper format defined and does not contain any error.

- Wrong geo-target:
  Targeting the wrong geo may look like a small mistake but has a bigger impact on the numbers, while checking the campaign setup Geo-targeting on both the server should be checked and should match. A scenario where ten cities are targeted on one ad server, the same ten cities should be on the other. One less or more can also create discrepancy easily.

- Third party redirecting ad call to another ad server:
  With the growth of technology, a lot of company tries to wrap the tag with another ad server which becomes a fourth party to the client is not recommended as more and more ad server enters the ecosystem the discrepancy automatically increases. Redirection of the third party should be done on a very important case and average percentage discrepancy should be considered in the first step.

- Slow web page and auto refresh web page:

  Today almost all the sites are dynamic and not static and every site owner tries to make the site full-fledged which eventually makes it heavy due to which it takes time to load even on a high-speed broadband. Imagine the condition of a site loading on a 2G network, just because of the slow web page the counting may differ from two different ad server, one may count once the call goes to the web server and the other may count once the ad loads on the site. But there could be a lot of case where the counting methodology is different but the site loading speed is fine which then reduces the counting issue as both fires but on a slight delay and at the end each server count its number, thereby saving the difference in number. So if the discrepancy happens, keep an eye on the site load speed to see if site loading speed is not hampering the counting methodology. The other reasons on the site could be of auto refresh on the site which is generally seen on sites which has real time data to show like the live cricket score or stock market data, etc. Due to the auto refresh, there could be multiple times when both servers may not count the impressions due to repetition very frequently and especially if the cache buster is missed on the tag then there would be a very high discrepancy.

MEDIA PLANNING

Definition:

Media planning is one important phase before the campaign execution takes place. It is a process in which a media plan or advertising strategy is created which consists of media platforms where the client's product will be advertised. These are best possible platforms according to the client product that they are looking to advertise. The plan consists of everything including the strategy and the deliveries commitment with the budget figure provided by the client at the time of briefing.

Media planning can be considered as a science as it involves both technical and business inputs from a media planner. The success of a media plan depends on a number of interrelated factors and correctness of the chosen strategy. As media planning being the foundation of success, every step should be questioned and analysed. A media plan can give impetus to the development of a product or service, be the starting point of success, but it certainly can also be turned against the product or service to meet them aggressively. Hence, every action in the media plan has a reaction, could be positive or negative too.

Principles of Media Planning:

It is not enough to know what types of advertising are available in the market and use each of them separately but it is necessary to be able to match all kinds of advertising and tools into a single media plan. Varity does not makes a perfect plan but relevant to the brief and audience targeting makes a perfect plan which makes client happy so it is always important to follow the strategy made earlier to the planning stage and take which is relevant. Media planning provides the most effective way to reach a target audience using the right advertising media. The task of media planning is the task of distribution of the advertising budget for different media and different platforms in the media, in order to obtain the largest and highest quality audience reach for the allocated money.

Four core principles of media planning are:

- Target Guidelines
- Compatibility Principle
- Optimization principles
- The principle of maximizing benefits

Stages of Media Planning:

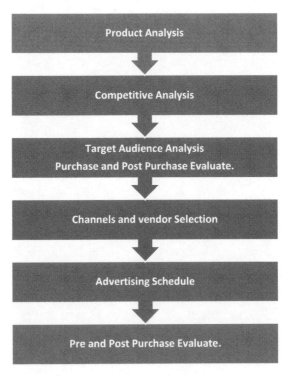

The ideal scenario is always to get the campaign brief from the client before starting to work on a media plan. A campaign or media brief consists of all the information that helps in all the stages of media planning.

NOTE: A Media or a campaign brief is a mandate before getting into the planning stage, if the client has not provided with the brief, please make sure to have a proper communication with the client and note down all what he says and create a brief using all the below elements and forward the same to the client and then start working on the planning stages. This activity ensures proper functioning of the planning stage as it is required in almost all the stages whereas the brief becomes the formal document between the client and the planner, anything missed or not understood correctly can be flagged by the client before you invest your time on wrong brief.

Below are the following elements that are seen in an ideal campaign brief:

- Definition of the target audience or target in the most explicit way possible. Demographic location, their psychology, their buying habits, age ... and even the role as a consumer, prescriber or buyer.
- Product definition - Differentiation, added value and the benefits to the consumer always treated from the point of view of its use, profitability, and life cycle.
- Characteristics and conditions of the potential market - Current situation, conditions of sale, total market volume, trends, etc.
- Competitive environment - Knowing the competition is critical. Not only brands and their market share but also trends and marketing strategies, advertising and promotion, as well as differences between leading products, pricing, image, and design, etc.
- Company data - Your mission, culture, principles and standards by which it is governed, its strategy of corporate identity, etc.
- Channel indication - It should be noted marketing channels, both their own and those of competitors.
- Advertising experiences and historical analysis - It is important to take into account the communication actions undertaken earlier, its objectives and what were the results.
- Objectives we want to accomplish - As mentioned earlier while setting targets it is essential to communicate the goals and marketing strategies of our company to establish the objectives of the different communication strategies.

- Key data about the budget - Although clients are often reluctant to communicate the budget, the fact is that it is essential to know which economic parameters must move the agency.
- Campaign duration – How long the campaign will run i.e. start and end date.

Now let's move on to the stages of media planning:

Product Analysis:

The first stage of every media plan should be to understand the product/ service that the advertiser is interested in promoting online. Without the knowledge of product, it's difficult to create a successful media plan as any or previous media plan won't work for every kind of product. The variation in the media plan as per the requirement is important and should be well taken care by the media planner. It is well observed that any successful media plan won't help create another success with the same but the chances of failure are high. The successful media plan may give you some idea or insight but following it blindly won't help.

Competitive Analysis:

Beautifully defined by Entrepreneur India -" A competitive analysis is a critical part of your company marketing plan. With this evaluation, you can establish what makes your product or service unique--and therefore what attributes you play up in order to attract your target market."

It can also be referred as a situation analysis in general and is the most important step before starting to work on a media plan. It is very important to analyse the product competition which helps in knowing the strong and the weak point in your product, looking at which a strategic media plan can be made. The competitive analysis includes analysis of competitor products, price, physical distribution i.e. service and promotional steps that they are taking in the market, etc. Hence, overall situation of competitors is analysed.

Target Audience Analysis:

After the understanding of the product and its competitors, the next important analysis is about the target audience i.e. the audience that we are looking to promote the product online. This stage is no less important or crucial as targeting the ads to the wrong audience definitely leads to failure and so detailed analysis on the target audience is worth spending time. The best scenario is to create two lists of target audience i.e. primary and secondary wherein primary being the apt audience whereas secondary being the expected target.

Important segments to be looked on while forming target audience for the campaign:

- Demographic profile - Includes age, gender, education, income, marital status, etc.
- Psychographic characteristics - Includes consumer thoughts, behavior, beliefs, interests, hobbies, etc.
- Buying Behavior - Brands that the consumer looks for, credit or debit card holder, quick in decision or takes time after viewing the product, etc.
- Geographic location - Consumer physical location is important. A local brand may look to advertise on smaller cities whereas bigger brands may look to target NRI's

Channel or Vendor Selection:

This stage is the action stage where channels and vendors are selected as per the campaign brief or objective. Channel includes Display, Social, Mobile, Search, Content, etc. whereas vendor selection includes the sites or apps. In this stage, all the sites with their traffic, cost, audience, etc. are evaluated which is then selected to complete the objective that the client or advertiser has asked for.

This process may include taking help from tools like comScore or tools that has sites analytics data.

Advertising Schedule:

Yes, it's very important to work on the schedule of the campaign within the timeframe of the campaign. If the campaign timeframe is January to July, a proper schedule has to be made keeping all the holidays, weekends, weekday, season, etc. in mind. The schedule includes the number of impressions in a day, week or monthly to be served to the target audience. It also includes the sponsorship day which has been booked with the vendors.

Factors to be kept in mind while creating a schedule-

- Seasonality - Season becomes important for a lot of products like food, clothes, tours, heating supplies, air condition, etc. Thereby considering the duration of the Campaign falls under which four quarter of the year is also important. If the product has no relation to the season then this factor can be ignored.

- Holidays and Special Days - On the positive side, if a product is launching before Christmas then advertising before the Christmas may boost the campaign success whereas on the negative side, on a holiday very fewer people come on the internet and go for tours or relax with family so advertising on a holiday may lead to grab less eye on the ad. Hence, while making the schedule, holidays and any special day should be well considered.

- Days - A lot of campaign doesn't work in weekends whereas a lot of works in weekends only, this evaluation or learning comes from the previous campaign and should be considered while making the schedule. You can always schedule your campaign for only weekday or weekend as per your requirement. The running on selected day is very easy to manage by using the feature called day parting. Also, a day like salary day is an important day for a lot of consumers to participate in online shopping.

- Hours - Which hour of the day campaign should run aggressively or be completely off can be also easily managed and is an important factor to be considered knowing your target audience may not be on the internet for the complete whole day. Like in night time it may not work for a lot of product so wasting impressions at night can be a waste of money so having time parting on the campaign could be beneficial always.

Purchase and Post Purchase Evaluate:

Media planning process ends with the start of this stage and moves into the execution phase where evaluation on both purchase plus post purchase is done. The role of the media planner doesn't end completely as in some cases selected vendor may not perform as per its target then the media plan may require some changes to achieve the overall objective which is taken care by a media planner only. The success of the advertising campaign is always a report card at the end.

The performance of the campaign is evaluated as per the reports, looking at which revision in the plan is made if required. The campaign is continuously analysed and optimized till it ends.

Post evaluation is done after the campaign ends. This is done in sync with operation team to share the exact numbers that have been delivered. Summary about the campaign which shows what worked and what didn't. It also has the success story with screenshots plus the audience reach and frequency details. The post evaluation can consist of all the information which can be beneficial for the client and can help the team for next campaigns as altogether it's a summary of learning made out of the campaign executed

The evaluation process considers below elements:

- Media targets
- Media Strategies
- Reach/Frequency
- Media tool selection
- Vendor selection
- Campaign Delivery
- Discrepancies
- Spends
- ROI
- Proof of execution i.e. screenshots

Challenges in Media Planning:

Media planning challenge is to understand the audience of the product or service and then find such sites which will emphasize their dignity. The selected space should be a space in which the product or service look natural and apt. Understanding of the product may not be very tough if proper download and communication are done with the client. This may initially take up the time but fortunately leads to a successful campaign; thereby understanding of the product is the most important before starting to work on a media plan.

Important parameters to be looked on while planning:

- Aims and Objective - What is the objective of the campaign, branding/ awareness or leads? Very important to be aware of the aim the client has.
- Target Audience - Depending on the client's product the target audience varies and should be considered primarily for a successful campaign. The vendors included in the plan should have the same target that we are looking for the client's product. Example: Advertising a business product like office 365 on a student website may not be the right target which will anyways lead to failure.
- An experience of previous similar campaigns - Experience from the previous campaign always helps in perfect planning, the experience out of previous campaigns provides a significant impact on preparing a media plan.
- Analysis of competitors - Always important to know what the brands competitor is doing, this also helps in media planning.
- Time frame - Definition of a clear start and end dates from the client is important. On the time frame of the campaign, if festivals, public holiday, weekends all needs to consider while making a media plan.
- Budget - Last but important is the budget of the campaign provided by the client. Before giving a start on the media plan, the budget needs to be divided into large sections like mobile, display, programmatic, video and sponsorship. Then after if the budget is too low and the objective is not awareness then sponsorship may not be the part of the plan and so on

MEDIA BUYING

Definition:

The buying of advertising space for the purpose of advertising from a company operating media properties is called media buying.

The cost of a media buy varies depending on the specific media property on which the buyer wants to advertise like the size of the ad space, the specific times at which the advertisements are to be displayed, Geo and other specific features of the advertising campaign.

Media buying is the purchase of advertising space in the media space. Buying print ads in newspapers, 30 second TV spots during prime time, billboards, plus buying slots on websites for banner ads is considered as media buying. Media buying requires some serious introspection as you should be aware of what exactly you are buying at what price. Prior detailed knowledge will help in closing the deal with the vendor at the lowest cost. The art of the media buy is in a state of flux as online media is growing and changing rapidly. The best approach could be a 10% of the complete budget of every plan in testing new vendors which will determine multiple options and the most effective for your brand.

Who are media buyers?

Media buyers are the one employed by advertising agencies and marketing to negotiate the purchase of advertising time or space on behalf of their clients. It may be digital media, newspapers or magazines, television, radio, websites, and social networks, or other media, such as billboards.

Points to be considered for smarter media planning:

- Refer to complete and accurate data:
  It is always wise to refer previous campaign data which helps in proper and perfect media buying. The cost can be easily negotiated looking at the previous performance. E.g. If in any previous campaign with the same vendor we did a fixed campaign, for which now we can calculate the eCPM looking at the delivery report, basis the market average CPM rate we can negotiate on the next fixed deal.

- Buy as per the metric that works for you:
  While efficiency is a key goal of any online media buying, every professional and every media campaign has unique goals. Find a metric that best correlates with the measurement of the value of your goal, if the goal is sales, then the buying can be done accordingly like one sale per thousand visits or directly on CPS (cost per sales) rather working on CPC or CPM

- Constantly test the impact of each data analysis to verify and substantiate their decisions:
  The performance of small tests in all major decisions can keep professionals on the right track as they evolve the media buying strategies. For example, if your agency or DSP platform decides to add another publisher content because data show that it can yield a better conversion rate, perform tests with and without the new editor, to know whether it will really add value.

- Be patient when analysing the changes of results based on guidance data:
  Perfecting based on insights derived from data campaigns and analysis results can take time. Evaluate how these results are crucial to your business, determine the cost and time you want to invest in finding these results and giving, to your campaign, a chance to prove or disprove the data.

- Negative results are still results and can be good:
  We all like to see positive results when testing the validity of a decision based on data. However, negative results can be either important or even more important. Identify inefficiency in a campaign and eliminate it is as valuable as finding what works best.

Media Buy Types:

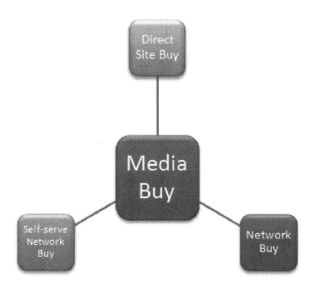

1. **Direct Site Buy**: This is when a single site is bought for serving the ads. This is costly as this is generally done when site takeover is bought i.e. site page will have only single advertiser ad but not necessarily it has to be fixed buy and can be normal ad space buying also, it's just the buying is done directly from the site representative and not via any third party or networks. This type of buying may lead to less rate as there is no third party involved but will consume a lot of time while planning for a campaign.

    Advantages:
    *   Visibility
    *   Ads run as per your choice
    *   Cost saving as per buying the same site via the third party
    *   Ability To Target Extremely Targeted Audiences e.g. if you buy sites like cartrade.com your targeting user will be auto interest, similarly you can buy sites depending on the user targeting that you need for your product

    Disadvantages:
    *   Consumes more time in planning
    *   Costly when compared to network buy

2. **Network Buy**: As the name says, in this the collection or network of sites are bought on which the ads will throw impressions, e.g. companies like tribal fusion or value click, etc. does this kind of display advertising. In this kind of buying the sites are bought as per categories like games, automotive, entertainment, shopping, etc.

   Buying collection of sites cost you less as compared to single buy but network buy is a blind buy where the advertiser don't get to know where exactly their ad is running as networks won't disclose the sites.

   Advantages:
   - Saves times in planning
   - Less cost as collection of sites are provided
   - Increased reach
   - Campaign is managed well, all you need to look is on the campaign report to see its performance
   - Flexible payment models, i.e. CPA, CPC, CPM, etc.

   Disadvantages:
   - Advertiser never gets to know where his ad is running – i.e. Visibility concerns
   - Discrepancy issues i.e. difference in reports between own and networks

3. **Self-serve Network Buy**: This media buying provides you with the means to manage your own account and allow you to come and go as you please. This buying is self-dependent buying, in this, you get an interface where you run your own campaign selecting the inventory as per your own requirement. E.g. Say you are an advertiser and you sign up with sitescount (A Self-Serve Advertising Platform) where you then create your campaign choosing the media type, costing, publishers, etc. The benefit of such buy is you are not dependent on any anyone and you can manage your campaign targeting, running dates, budget consumption, capping, etc. at your end.

   Advantages:
   - Independent decision

- Saves time w.r.t buying inventory as today the interface provided by companies are very user-friendly
- Cost management as per your needs, generally cost you less than other two kinds of buying

Disadvantages:
- Saves money but consumes time in trafficking the campaign initially
- You can't get bonus impressions i.e. value ad
- Screenshots are difficult to get i.e. proof of delivery is a challenge

Process of media buying:

Before we get into the process of media buying, let's know the three important aspects of media buying.

- Networking – Relationship with right contact is very important in media buying. The buying process goes smoothly if you have a good relation in the media industry. At times you can close the deal over a call due to relationship only.
- Awareness & Investigation – Awareness about the new vendors is mandate in media buying as more you know what is going in industry it makes it easy to plan and strategies taking all new and old options. Another important aspect of media buying is never rely on other words but always investigate yourself about the media vendor and take decisions.
- Negotiate – Negotiation in media buying is a primary part and also a media buyer should be capable enough of convincing media vendors to not only low the rates but also gives value ad and bonuses when required.

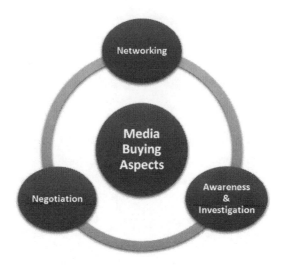

Let's divide the process of media buying into five different steps for better understanding and clear view -

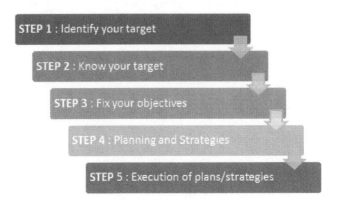

STEP 1: Identify your target -
Before you plan to buy the ad space, you need to know your target market. To do this the best approach is to create a profile with questions like –

- Who are you trying to reach?
- Who is your target market?
- What is their age?
- Male or Female?
- Income, etc.

STEP 2: Know your target -

Once you've identified your target market, it's time to do some market research. It's important to understand the consumer behavior of those that you are targeting. You can do your own research, which is called primary research or you can also depend on secondary research which may not be that accurate as primary but would help in understanding your target perfectly.

Knowing your target is very important before you start as it helps a lot in catching the exact users, like identifying where you will find your target market. This will help in placing a media buy that is effective and performs by achieving your identified objectives. Research can help you in doing this. Research can also provide you with the information on what your competitors are doing and where they are going to reach the audience you are trying to reach.

STEP 3: Fix your Objectives

When you are done with all the research and have some proper insight about your target audience, the next step to work on is setting up the objectives so that you get to know your success level in achieving your target.

STEP 4: Planning and Strategies

What can be after when you have identified, researched your target and have set the objectives - It's now about planning and making some perfect strategies to obtain the objectives within the budget and in time! This planning does not include of final plan that is sent to the client but planning on holding the media vendors that have been well suited to catch the target audience that we are looking for. The listing of all possible vendors are done keeping the cost limit in mind.

STEP 5: Execution

Now you have your plan and all strategies in hand, it's time to get to real work. Your first step is to begin to contact the media vendors you have identified and starts negotiating your media buy rates. Make sure you negotiate rates and ask for bonuses or add-ons that they are willing to give you if you choose to go with them. With all these, do keep the eyes on your budget, your calendar and, most importantly, keep track of important deadlines and objectives that you have made while listing the vendors. You are free to make changes and adjust your plans if the requirement is there as this is not your final plan.

NOTE: Media buying primarily goal is to help in buying ad spaces at best rest but the buying model may differ, some media buyers make yearly deal and some work as per campaign requirement. The yearly deals helps you to crack best rates but this is beneficial only if you have some clarity on the budget spend of the year, if the budget of clients for the year is high then it is good to go for yearly deals else campaign specific deals are no bad if you are a perfect media buyer with sound knowledge of the market and rates.

OPTIMIZATION

"Please get the campaign optimized", "scale up your campaign", etc. are such liners that is heard usually. So let's know what does that mean and what optimization in online advertising is?

The word Optimization itself defines it's meaning whether it be an advertising field or any other. When you look at the definition of Optimization it says *"to make as effective, perfect, or useful as possible"* or *"to get the most out of"*. Same as what it defines in online advertising too, we optimize every campaign that we work on so that we can take out the best of it and serve the Ads at the best level making it cost effective too!

Optimization means finding an alternative with the most cost effective or highest achievable performance under the given constraints, by maximizing desired factors and minimizing undesired ones, meaning – It is natural that some ads perform better than other ads. It means that some ads generate more revenue, more clicks, more conversions, a higher click-through ratio, or a higher conversion ratio. With this feature, you can always choose to display the better performing ads more often and this increases the return over investment (ROI) for better ads and raises a flag on poor ads that should be revised /improved or any changes that may help the specific Ad to perform better too!

Optimization requires changes at every step and these changes help advertisers save money by reducing wasted, ineffective impressions and ensuring that the right message is delivered to the right consumers, but the changes cannot be any step as there are some rules to be followed for correct way of optimizing online branding campaigns.

Optimization seems to be an easy one, but needs a lot of strategy, analytic, common sense, and ideas and of course a lot of experience can be a best help. It does come up with the experience as there is no hard and fast rule. There can be different tips and factors on which optimization can be done.

Factors considered for optimizations are:

- Clicks - Ads with more clicks than other ads in the same period will be served more often.
- Conversion – Ads with more conversions than other ads in the same period will be served more often.
- CTR (click through rate) – Ads with a higher CTR than other ads in the same period will be served more often.
- Sites having higher CPC but almost no conversion or less should be blocked.
- Cookie Users - Almost 30% of users don't accept cookies, so not including the 70% users may hamper the campaign performance. Targeting the cookie user will bring better performance too. Today the technology has made possible to also target the user who does not accept cookies but including both will always boost the campaign performance, so always include both cookied and non-cookied users.
- Budget (min cost) – The budget that has been allocated for every publisher on which the sites has to be served on, it can be changed as per the requirements.
- Frequency cap – If no capping is applied, the campaign delivery goes normally but it's an important factor which can be used for optimization. Serving the same ad to same user may irritate the user and this can result into negative impact over the brand. Ideal frequency cap per user per day is 3, you can always change as per your campaign requirement.

An accurate and up-to-date optimization requires a continuous stream of input data. The ad optimization feature takes into account of all the data that an ad has when it is served across all zones. Thus, it is a holistic approach. Optimization is done for the ad, based on its whole performance in all zones that it is linked to and not just within any specific zone.

As already mentioned there is no such hard and fast rule to make the campaign successful in one click. Every Ad server has their own rules and settings to follow for better optimization. But one thing is common with every optimization rule is TESTING, the first phase of optimization is testing phase where some budgets and impressions are spent for testing purpose and second phase called as OPTIMIZATION phase where actual optimization for the campaign is done. Normally ad server delivers 1000 impressions on every publisher (completely depends on server to server) so that it can catch up the pace and after looking up the performance and response the optimization is done accordingly. It's true that it totally depends upon campaign to campaign, testing can be very small at low budget campaigns which indirectly means now the campaign response totally depends upon the probability of catching the user (w.r.t CPA/CPL campaigns), sometimes 100 impressions get us a conversion and sometimes lot of testing don't help, so as mentioned optimization has no rule to make you sure of giving success but yes the probability can be low and high always.

Simple to follow, If the campaign is performing fine we make no changes and if the campaign performance is degrading we make changes according to the target of the campaign, rather by increasing or decreasing the CPM or other factors discussed above.

Optimization is totally a trial method, you become expert with experience only. At times some or the other way it works and at times nothing works and you be clueless that why the campaign is not scaling up. But yes mostly checking all the factors and rectifying it makes the campaign work well. Optimization is the most important step in campaign execution and cannot be ignored, if ignored campaign may under deliver or may over-deliver also.

Three major components of optimization that you need to always consider:

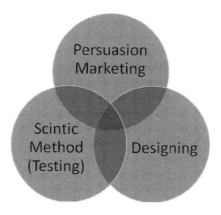

- Persuasion marketing - Right message to right target at right time is a mandate and should be closely looked at the campaign delivery.
- Experience design - Attractive creative with apt content is very important, this is called creative optimization where we optimize the creative as per campaign delivery results.
- Scientific Method - Continuous testing is very important so apply the known methods to optimize but keep a check to see if the action is working or not. This method is called as scientific as the steps taken are basic the science behind the ad server algorithms.

Creative Optimization: Now what's this? It is also a part of optimization step or say factor. When you change the non performing creative with performing or new ones it is called creative optimization as creative can also be a major reason for low performance, so changing creative also leads to better performance of the campaign.

Over and under delivery of campaign: Solution in Optimization process!

Before I give up some solutions or points, just wanted to let you know that optimizing the campaign is a real time job and changes required are always as per the scenario and the campaign type (CPA, CPM or CPC, etc.) The solution cannot be same for every campaign and it differs with respect to buying model.

The below points are the general solutions that are always processed when campaign is under performing or over performing:

- The first and the foremost thing to be done is check the campaign setup properly that everything is set up as per requirement or not.
- Check the targeting that the campaign is targeted to right users or not.
- Increase the priority of the campaign if it's too low. This won't affect much but can be helpful at times.
- Increase the budget if the campaign is under-delivery or decreases the budget if the campaign is over-delivered.

- Make the changes with the running date, it affects the campaign directly. You can always increase the end date if the campaign is over delivering or vice versa.
- Expand the targeting for under delivery cases.
- Also, check the frequency capping if applied. Frequency cap set to 1 may lead to under delivery. It completely depends on the inventory that you have.
- Make the changes with the CPM, or CPC, increase or decrease as per the campaign requirement. Brings quick effect!
- Last but the least - If all the setup and everything seem to be good, you can get the IO revised.

Points to be kept in mind before starting to optimize:

- Avoid number of changes:
  Making number of changes will lead to more downfall of the campaign performance, it shouldn't be like trying everything in and waiting to see what works and what not, this will only result in a lot of wasted media spend. There should always be minimum change and the best practice is to plan initially as per the campaign and then make changes.

- Be patient:
  Always be patient while optimizing the campaign, don't expect the fast result, and observe the campaign looking at the report after making any changes.

- Abrupt decisions:
  Another thing to be kept in mind always is please don't make any abrupt decisions while optimizing; it shouldn't be too before or too late. There are times people start making changes so as to get the best benefit out of campaign and reduce the extra waste but it's not the correct way to handle the campaign. As already discussed that you need to be patient, the campaign cannot start delivering in one go?

TRACKING

What is tracking?

Track is "footprints or other marks left by an animal, person, or vehicle, etc." and tracking is catching the desired thing with the help of tracks.

In online advertising TRACKING plays the main role in leading you to success. It actually plays a vital role in online business! Earlier only some information of a user were tracked but today any information that you put up on websites can be easily tracked, social network sites are playing a quite bigger role or help in tracking accurate information. The purpose for all of this online snooping is nothing but a help in spending the money at the right place i.e. in online advertising it's about showing up the right ads to the right person so that the chances to get a response becomes more than expected. For e.g. if you show the kids related ads to an old aged user will be of no use and vice versa.

We will be discussing in detail about tracking, Lets divide them into two parts so that we can learn and know them clearly.

- Ad Tracking
- Web Tracking

Ad Tracking:

So when you talk about Ad tracking, it's completely about your ad that you are showing up and expecting some responses like clicks, sales or any actions, etc., now why do we track them? The answer is only because you want to know which path you are going, is it a success path or a failure path - precisely it's about knowing how much profit it is bringing to you. And always remember advertisers use the results of ad tracking to estimate the return on investment (ROI) of advertising, and to also to refine advertising plans for better performance.

Ad tracking always helps you in making comparison, testing new advertising ideas on a small scale before investing too much time or money on a full-fledged campaign - all together helping you to get the success.

Purpose:

Knowing about the Ad tracking you will get the idea that why do we need tracking but still to be more clear and exact below shown pictorial representation or flow chart will give you one of the purposes of Ad Tracking.

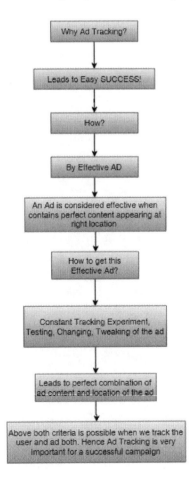

The tracked data ultimately helped you to achieve an effective ad so that you can capture right audience. It is very clear that if you don't track how the user is interacting with your ad or track what your visitors are doing on your website, how many visitors came to your site through a particular ad campaign, how many visitors converted into buyers, your ROI, etc., you cannot be certain if a particular ad campaign is worth continuing or not. Hence any kind of tracking is very important and should not be ignored. It may cost the advertiser some extra penny but at end the result will eventually hide the cost spent on tracking.

Ten important metric that every campaign should track

There are number of aspects for analysing your Ad performance which should be tracked.

Those are:

- Number of Clicks
- Number of Sales
- Number of Actions
- Total Value of Sales
- Cost of Campaign
- Total Profit or Loss
- CPC, or
- CPA
- Cost Per Sale
- ROI

Tracking all these aspects will let you know about the campaign stats which help you in making the changes if required! In the above ROI is the most important factor which accounts all your costs and compares that to the profit you made from the ad to come up with a percentage that indicates how successful your ad has been.

Web Tracking:

Web tracking is a practice by which websites identify, and collect information about users and their behavior. There are number of ways by which web tracking can be done. Earlier the forms of tracking were:

- Browser Fingerprinting - collects not just browser data but also data about how you type--things like your typing speed and typing patterns.
- Etags - Entity tag allows caches to be more efficient, and saves bandwidth, as a web server does not need to send a full response if the content has not changed.
- Visited link colouring
- Via Cache

These are normally not used as they started to become threat to privacy!

Web tracking is highly prevalent today as it's a great help to the website owner as well as to the advertisers as it helps in providing the desirable functionality, site analytics and also targeted advertisements. The web tracking is at its best when larger browsing profiles but other way (user) it's a threat to privacy and loss of data.

Before we understand the procedure of tracking let's know the two basic functionality of a tracker which helps the tracking functionality possible.

The two major functionality of a tracker are:

- STORAGE - The tracker has the ability to store a unique identifier on the user's machine
- COMMUNICATION - The tracker has the ability to communicate with the unique identifier plus visited sites plus the tracker's domain e.g.doubleclick.net.

Working:

Let's talk about the normal working of the trackers that how they exactly work and how are they helpful in catching the users.

Below is the simple diagrammatic representation of the working:

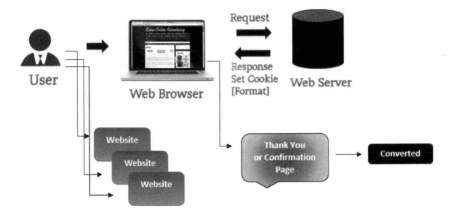

STEPS:

- The user opens any browser (IE, Chrome or Mozilla) where he enters the URL of his desired landing page, e.g. ebay.com, he opens the eBay site.
- The Browser requests the eBay web server for the content of the web page.
- Web server replies back with the content and also a command to set the cookie, the format of the cookie can be defined by the web server too.
- The browser responses with the cookie detail to the server.
- There can be two possibilities: either the user buys something i.e. a conversion is tracked or just checks out something and leaves away from the site.
- The user now moves to different sites the same day or may be a different day, he will be shown the relevant ad (if running or live) of the product he checked on eBay. This is called tracking the user which increases the possibility of being converted if not converted at first instance.

What is the difference between Static Pixel Tracking and Dynamic Pixel Tracking?

SNo.	STATIC PIXEL TRACKING	DYNAMIC PIXEL TRACKING
1.	Static pixel does not change.	A dynamic pixel can be made to change by an outside influence.
2.	It does not require any extra information to be appended.	It requires dynamic information to be appended when the pixel is written
3.	A static pixel is simply used to collect data like no. of views or conversion or clicks	A dynamic pixel is collects the data which static pixel does but also gathers more information like order ID, Shipping city, region, buyer ID, order Total, etc. These values are pulled dynamically which can later be used for tracking or retargeting the user accordingly.
4.	Time consuming in the implementation, w.r.t creative	Saves a lot of time as you don't have to upload every single creative as dynamic implementation will play the role using the macros
5.	Accurate as less use of technology	There are possibilities of wrong reports due to small issue may cause collection of wrong data.

What is Client Based Tracking and Server Based Tracking?

To know the tracking process let's know the roots of tracking procedures so that the process becomes crystal clear. There are two primary ways to track transaction flow from the moment of first click to the point where conversion takes place. Either you are tracking users via cookies on their browser or doing a server call to store a unique identifier.

The two ways, formerly called as:
- Client Based Tracking
- Server Based Tracking

Client Based Tracking:

Now, what is client based, seems like all the tracking done at client side is client based tracking then who is the client here? The client here is no one but the user's browser. Client based tracking is completely based on cookies that are stored on user's browser. It relies on storing information on the actual user's computer by placing a cookie in the user's browser when an advertisement is clicked. If the user reaches the conversion page (final sale or lead), a tracking pixel that was placed on the conversion page sends the cookie information back to the tracking platform, recording a conversion for the proper affiliate. This type of tracking is the most common technique used and most commonly used by the advertisers as embedding advertiser tracking pixel on the conversion page is the only thing required to do. The ease of setup for advertisers and low requirement of technical savvy make client-based tracking an excellent solution for many networks.

Server Based Tracking:

Another type of tracking which is done is server based tracking. This kind of tracking is totally independent of cookies and as also called as cookie-less tracking. Also don't get confused by server to server tracking as it's another name to server based tracking.

Server-based tracking requires nothing to be placed on the user's computer. This feature of this tracking method makes it best as no conversion is lost even when the user disables the cookie on its browser. It works by generating and storing a unique identifier of some kind when a user clicks a tracking link or generates an ad impression. All the information regarding the user, the advertiser or the site is stored in the server with a unique identifier associated with it. The unique identified can be the transaction ID or site ID. The ID gets passed through the tracking URL to the server hosting the offer landing page and is stored by the advertiser. This identifier is passed through as a variable throughout the conversion funnel. When the transaction is complete, the ID is passed back to the affiliate tracking server by calling a "Post back URL" at the time of conversion.

Post back URL looks like http://domain.com/sid=123456.

Also server to server tracking do not use third party cookies like client based tracking do but they make use of first party cookie as they are normally never blocked by any user. The use of this cookie comes when someone do not get converted at that instant but may be after a week, than this local cookie helps in catching the user.

What is Static and Dynamic click tracker?

What is a click tracker?

A click tracker is a tagged landing page URL which helps to track the number of clicks happened on a banner, link, email, or any form of ad which is clickable. With the help of a click tracker, the success of an ad can be easily evaluated.

S No.	Static Click Tracker	Dynamic Click Tracker
1.	Even if the click tracker line item is not live, the tracker will redirect you to landing page but won't track numbers in the report	This redirects to a blank page and also does not record any numbers
2.	Static click tracker has two status i.e. Archived and unarchived. Unarchived keeps the click tracking live, one archived the tracking URL won't work	Dynamic click tracker has three status option i.e. Active, Inactive and Archived.
3.	In static click tracker we need to manually add the destination URL	In dynamic click tracker the destination URL is automatically inserted into the ad tag
4.	Example: https://ad.doubleclick.net/ddm/clk /000000040;131020420;d?https:// masterpass.com/#en-in	Example: https://ad.doubleclick.net/ddm/ clk/0000000;131020420;l

The below error fires when dynamic click tracking is not set to active:

HttpFox							
▶ Start ❌ Stop ✖ Clear 🔍 double			☑ Autoscroll				
Started	Time	Sent	Received	Method	Result	Type	URL
00:00:32.848	0.714	469	274	GET	400	text/html	https://ad.doubleclick.net/ddm/clk/304849351;131020420;l

The below image shows the firing when dynamic tracker is firing without any error:

What is Post click tracking?

The term post-click tracking, abbreviated as PCT, includes a tracking method that measures the click path of a visitor to a website after clicking on an ad. When a banner ad is clicked, the post click tracker gets activated and starts to capture the activity of the user. PCT helps to evaluate the user profile plus its potential towards buying the product, it also helps in easy tracking of the conversions.

Two forms of post click tracking:

1. Sessions based tracking
2. Cookie based tracking

What is Session based tracking and cookie based tracking?

Session based tracking is a tracking method where the collected data only refers to the current session of the user. Once the user closes his browser or remains inactive, the trackable data become of no use or assigned. Example: If a visitor makes an order in the same session the conversion is counted else if the visitor makes the conversion the next day or after the active session the conversion does not appear in the analysis or report.

Cookie based tracking is a method in which a file on a user's computer is stored which consists of detailed information about the user and his activity is saved. Cookie helps to track and identify the user perfectly which helps to track down the activity of the user after clicking on the banner ad. Example: If a user clicks on a banner and lands to the landing page where he selects a product but does not buy it in the same instant, the same user comes back to the landing page by any other means and buys the product. This conversion is counted and remains associated with the same user. Such kind of conversion is called 'Delayed Conversion'. Generally the cookie generation is set to 30 days for default.

What is Conversion tracking?

It is the tracking of successful completion of any action on a website by the user, like purchase, sign-up, or any action which is considered as a final goal for the client.

The purpose of conversion tracking is to know the success rate of your campaign or say product. It can be used to track number of actions like:

- Purchase
- Sign-ups
- Submission of E-mail addresses
- Goal Page
- Any event which can help to know the success of the campaign can be tracked.

What is Conversion Pixel?

A conversion pixel is generally a 1x1 image fired through a short line of code which is placed on your confirmation page or thank you page. It fires whenever any user reaches to the confirmation page which helps in capturing data of number of converted users.

Who are Converted users?

Users that have crossed the confirmation page are the converted users and the ones who reached to the website but didn't purchase or did any successful completion of conversion event they fall into imprinted pool and are called imprint users or also non-converted users.

Example:
    <img src = "http://www.knowonlineadvertising.com/conversion/ab1323cd234 h531Z" width = 1 height = 1 border = 0>
    *It is not a general syntax but one of the forms of conversion code.

What is Conversion rate?

The conversion rate is the one which tells about the conversion success of the campaign. It is the number of conversions divided by the number of impressions served. Higher is the conversion rate higher is the success of a campaign.

Formula of conversion rate is: number of conversions/number of Impression X 100

Short and Simplified Working:

The simple working of conversion tracking starts when the user clicks on an ad or a banner, clicking on the ad fires a cookie on the user's browser which keeps the record of the time, site, banners, placement, etc.(information that can be required to capture the conversion). These records help in tracking the conversion if the user is not converted at the same time but gets converted next time when it comes directly to the website, this conversion recorded goes to the agency/ network who gave the ad impression.

How does conversion tracking work? (STEP WISE)

Assuming you, the advertiser, has placed our conversion tracking code at the end of the ordering process (for example: "Thank You" page), the process will follow these steps:

- View Ad
  A visitor views the ad on 1st January; the ad server simply records an impression on January 1st.

- Click on Ad
  A visitor clicks on the ad and begins browsing the advertiser's store on January 1st. The ad server records a click on January 1st and a cookie is created to track conversions and it could last up to 30 days (default) after the click.

- Purchase
  This visitor eventually makes a purchase on January 1st and gets to the "Thank You" page that contains the conversion tracking code. The

ad server records this conversion and awards it to the original click. A zone is also credited if the clicked ad was served via that zone.

- View-Through Conversion
  If a purchase was made but there was no recorded click, our ad server would record it as a view-through conversion.

What is View-Through conversion and Click-Through Conversion?

The conversion which is based on impressions and not after clicking on the ad is view-through conversion i.e. a user sees a banner and then later completes a conversion on the website by directly going to the website will be considered as view through conversion. It is beneficial for branding campaigns which are impression based and measures the conversions where user saw the ad but didn't click.

Click-Through Conversion is different of view-through as it is based on clicks and not just views, the conversion which happens after clicking on the ad whether the same moment or even after the user comes directly to the website and converts but has previously clicked on the ad will be considered as click-through conversion.

What is Piggybacking?

Definition:

The general definition is "carry by or as if by means of a piggyback" – In phrase: "I'll piggyback you the rest of the way". This means a support or a help to surpass to reach your destination.

Definition in terms of Advertising:

It refers to the use of a single container tag (also called universal or master tag) which redirects to other additional tags that are not placed directly on the site. Basically, it's a technique by which the actual tag fires without directly implementing on the page which ensures there is no data stolen from the client site maintaining the security.

General Example to understand piggyback concept:

- Using someone's shoulder to achieve something (raw example)
- Embedding the names of popular brands or companies into the hidden meta-data of a Web page in order to rank high up on a search engine's results page
- Gaining access to a restricted communications channel by using the session another user already established.
- Reaching to a destination with someone's help (hidden)

Live example of piggybacking:

Here Container tag is of ATLAS, where the pixel tagged is of Tribal Fusion, MathTag and Turn.

```
function AT__tags(){
  try{
    var tags =newArray();
    var imgs =newArray();
    tags
=['https://pixel.mathtag.com/event/img?mt__id=xxxxxx&mt__adid=xx
xxxx&v1=&v2=&v3=&s1=&s2=&s3=','http://a.tribalfusion.com/i.cid?c=xx
xxxx&d=00&page=landingPage','http://d.turn.com/r/dft/id/Xxxxxxxxx
xxxxxxxxxxxxxxxxxxxxxxxxxx'];
    for(var i =0; i < tags.length; i++){
      imgs[i]=newImage();
      imgs[i].src = tags[i];
    }
    this.csk ='Test';
  }catch(e){
    this.csk ='Error';
  }
}
```

Scenario: We need to place publisher pixel on client's LP for optimization or say retargeting but client is not allowing to implement the third party pixels due to global or security reasons

Solution: We can piggyback the publisher pixels like you can see in the above code for Tribal, Turn or mathtag pixel within an atlas container code

Result: Cookie pool is being formed at publisher end, thereby they can optimize and retarget the interested users. Client is also happy as they were not asked to put the pixels directly on the site

This is all about piggybacking!

Quick Points on piggybacking:

1. it's a technique which helps in retargeting the users
2. This is done by adding the actual action tag on a container tag which is then implemented on the client page
3. The implementation is same as normal tagging
4. This ensures the security of data, the publisher won't be able to steal data from client page i.e. user's pool, etc.

Difference between Piggybacking and Retargeting:

S. No.	Piggybacking	Retargeting
1.	It's a technique which helps in retargeting the users	It's a method which helps in catching the interested users
2.	This is done by adding the actual action tag on a container tag which is then implemented on the client page	The concept uses the data collected by piggybacking
3.	The implementation is same as normal tagging	The method is same for all, whether the data is collected via piggybacking or via directly
4.	This ensures the security of data, the publisher won't be able to steal data from client page i.e. user's pool, etc.	This ensures appropriate targeting

What is First, Second and Third Party Data?

It is tracking which helps to collect different forms of data and the same data is then used for running a successful campaign. There are majorly three forms of data that are collected – First, Second and Third party data. Let's know them in detail below:

First Party Data:

Who other can be first within different parties then you yourself, YES first party data is YOUR data and the data can include all the user data e.g. Behavior, Demo, Interests, etc.

These are the cookie-based data that you collect from your own website which can later be used to re target. Of all the data first party data is considered to be the most valuable as these data are from your own customers who lands to your website searches for some information which indirectly means the most interested and exact users. Another the best part about this data above accuracy is 'Free of cost' available to you as it is your own data only.

First party data is the most powerful data especially when synched up with an online ad campaign as the users targeted are the most accurate ones, thus concludes if someone is not making use of first party data then it is not indirectly but directly losing money thereby affecting ROI. These data are generally stored in CRM, loyalty program database or site analytic tools. Always remember there is no difference between publisher first party data and advertiser first party data because when a publisher collects its data it's his first party data whereas when an advertiser collects its data via its own site it's his first party data but yes when we talk about first party data it's generally the advertiser data which is of their customers and can be useful retargeting them whereas there is no use of publisher data (reader's data) directly in running an ad campaign

E.g. Microsoft as a client saves its customer data which is nothing but their first party data

Advantages:

- Accurate
- Free of Cost
- Future is always safe i.e. no privacy debates as for third party data

Second Party Data:

Second Party data is not well known like first party or third party data but is quite useful when used. It is actually a first party data that you get directly from the source (publisher). i.e. if we take the first party data from another source like any other website will become a second party data to us as the first party for us is our own data, similarly, if we share our own first party data to someone, that will become the second party to the one we have shared. Let me explain this with an example:

E.g. Suppose Microsoft has its own data which is their first party and is looking for some more data which if they tie up with someone (formal agreement) like with eBay, the same first party data of eBay will be considered as second party data for Microsoft which they can use to re target the potential users.

Second party data is new as compared to other two data but has almost same potential like first party and third party data. The second party data isn't usually commoditized, but can often work out an arrangement or deal with trusted partners who are willing to share their customer data with you (and vice versa) and by doing this both expand their data pool whilst maintaining some exclusivity.

Advantages:

- Less Accurate then first party but is still quite relevant to the product
- Helps in increasing the ROI

Third Party Data:

This data is a generalized data collected from different websites and is sold to them who are looking for more data. There are many companies who work in data collection and selling by which they run their complete business. The famous ones are Bizo, DataLogix, BluKai, etc.

The data collected is fragmented into channels like Auto, Female-centric, Sports, Entertainment, Tech, etc. The major disadvantage about this data is that it is available to competitors also so there is no unique targeting that is being done but still targeting the large scale of potential users is much better than targeting the unknown or categorized users. It also helps in removing the bot traffic as the data provided are filtered and clean

They generally use cookies to track users across the web and build individual profiles based on their activity and also buy data in large scale from publishers and are then filtered, also some companies make use offline sources to form accurate data. Though the competition is increasing these third party data providers use different ways to form perfect data for their clients.

Advantage:

- You can data as per your requirement or targeting
- Mass data provider
- Filters bot traffic

TARGETING

Definition:

Targeting is defined as selection of an object of attention or attack. Same is what it means in online advertising as we target our specific users (attack) as per the requirement of the campaign. Targeting is about catching the right user at the right time at right place so that the output coming out of it should be maximum.

Targeted Advertisement – It is an advertisement that is shown only to users exhibiting specific attributes or in a specific context or at a particular time of day.

In online industry targeting is a big world and is divided into sub parts:

- Contextual Targeting: Contextual targeting is a form of targeting that the ad servers use to target a user for showing ad units based on the context of the page they are viewing.
- Semantic Targeting: A type of contextual targeting that also incorporates semantic techniques to understand page meaning and/ or sentiment.
- Behavioral Targeting: Behavioral targeting is a form of targeting that ad server and ad networks use for targeting users based on their online behavior.
- Audience Targeting: A method that enables advertisers to show an ad specifically to visitors based on their shared behavioral, demographic, geographic and/or techno graphic attributes. Audience targeting uses anonymous, non-PII data.

- Geographic Targeting: The targeting of users as per zip code, area code, city, DMA, state, and/or country is called as geographic targeting.
- Creative Retargeting: A method that enables advertisers to show an ad specifically to visitors that previously were exposed to or interacted with the advertisers" creative.
- Site Retargeting: This targeting enables advertisers to show an ad specifically to previous site visitors.
- Time-based Targeting: Time- based parting can be divided into parts: time parting – this parting enables the ad to appear on certain time in a day while another is dayparting – this parting enables the ad to appear on certain days of the week.
- Demographic Targeting: The targeting of users on the basis of demographic information such as age, gender and income etc. is called as demographic targeting.

We will study in detail about some common forms of targeting that are used in online advertising.

Retargeting

Definition:

Retargeting is a method which enables the website owners to "re-attract" the previous visitors to their site. The concept of retargeting primarily focuses on increasing the conversions. Most of the times the users visits the site but does not participate in any call for action and leave the site, so retargeting tool or concept keeps the track of those visitors and follow them throughout the web. By doing so, when those visitors surf the web, the ad of the websites which the user recently visited is displayed to them, which most often compels the user to again visit the site.

Retargeting ensures that advertising infrastructure is utilized in the best possible way. Media gets spent on the people who have already visited the website and have shown interest in the past. This helps the marketers achieve high return on Investment or we can say greater chances of getting a conversion. Every time the customer sees the retargeting ads it generates the interest to visit the site again which increases the click through rates and conversions.

Concept of Retargeting believes in:

- Right Ad to Right People.
- Right Ad at Right Place.

Basic Working:

Retargeting is a cookie-based technology which involves the use of a tag, usually a JavaScript code. This Tag enables the marketers to follow the users all over the web.

A small JavaScript code is placed in the footer of the website. This code, also known as pixel is placed in such a manner that it remains unnoticed by the site visitors and also doesn't affect the performance of the site. Whenever a new visitors hits the web page, the code generates a random cookie which is placed in the user's browser. This cookie is helpful in tracking the user throughout the web. Now, when this cookied visitor surf the web, retargeting provider serve the ads of your website or product, which ensures that ads are served to only to people who had earlier visited your site.

Types of Retargeting:

1. Search Retargeting: This is most commonly used form of retargeting which focuses on searching the users through search engine on the basis of the keywords searched by them which are relevant to the sites data.
2. Site Retargeting: Site Retargeting focuses on the users that have already visited the website. This is done by tagging all the users who visit the site and then through the tag they can be followed throughout the web.
3. SEM/SEO Retargeting: This form of retargeting targets the individuals on the basis of the keywords which they use to reach to the website.
4. Email Retargeting: Email Retargeting focuses on the users on the basis of the actions they take in response to your email. User's interaction with the email program is the basis of targeting the users.
5. Contextual Retargeting: This form of retargeting targets those individuals who visit the site which have almost same data as your site.

6. Engagement Retargeting: This is least used form of retargeting which targets individuals who have interacted with distributed content like Facebook page, video, online game.

Best Practices:

*   Retargeting becomes more effective if the site visitors are grouped on the basis of the priority of items they were looking for. E.g.: the user looking for a travel bag, or rented house should be retargeted first as compared to the user looking for some luxury item like camera or jewellery. (Here priority is based on the need, someone who is looking for a house is a necessity)
*   We should try and avoid showing ad to the customer who has recently purchased that very product.
*   Avoid showing same ad for longer period.
*   Retargeting ad should contain "call-to-action" button which should directly take the user to the desired page upon clicking.

Limitation:

*   Retargeting can guaranty to increase the rate of conversion but it cannot attract new visitors to the site. So, in order to get the best out of retargeting it's important to follow practices like content marketing, AdWords and targeted display which helps in driving more traffic to the site. So, with this combination marketers can achieve higher return on Investment.
*   "Advertising-stalking" is currently effective, but also has a negative effect because the aggressive advertising may cause the user rejection. In general it is recommended that each month the user is shown the retargeting ad 7 to 12 times so that the user does not see the same (sometimes boring) ads multiple times.

Retargeting strategies basis User profile:

User Profile	Description	Strategy/Tactics	Bid price
Window shoppers	Just checked the homepage and did not view and detail page or product page	Show branding banner, Increase brand awareness and try to create confidence in the brand.	Low
Interested on the Product	User has visited the product detail pages Tried some of the product did not enter the shopping cart	Retarget with the same product he cancelled and also show some relevant product of the same brand	The bid could be medium or high depending on the user interest level but yes definitely bid cannot be low for such users
Prospective Buyer (60% convinced)	User did product comparison, entered the shopping cart but did not buy	Highlight the product and its Service or additional features. Best to show some case studies if any in regard to the product	High
Purchase Terminators (90% convinced)	User did all the comparison, moved from shopping cart to filling of payment details but cancels in between	Show banners with free shipping, or discount banners	High
Converted User	Has already made the purchase	Don't leave behind the converted user but bucket them to show other or relevant product ads like the set of baseball ball if he bought a baseball bat. If not the product convince to like FB page or follow at Twitter/ Instagram, etc.	Mid–High, depending on the time frame he took to purchase the previous product

Remarketing

Just like Retargeting, we have another targeting concept called 'remarketing'. The working process is same as retargeting, all it differs by is that it is often done using direct mail or email and Google has named its retargeting concept as remarketing.

The official definition of remarketing according to Google:

Remarketing can help people who have previously visited specific pages on your website to accomplish while visiting other sites in the Google Display Network.

Usually people visit the websites but not always indulge in any actions. So, remarketing is a technique which aims at reaching out to those people who have previously visited the website. Remarketing is done by showing ads to the potential customers all across the web.

In more simple words, it's bringing back to customer who visited your site but did not perform any transaction.

This is something very similar to retargeting (but not same), as remarketing also uses the concept of small piece of code known as tag, added to each page of the website which helps to catch the users whenever they visit the site, the code helps to track the users and ultimately helping to form a remarketing lists using which they can be reached all across the web.

Types of Remarketing:

1. Remarketing for Display Network: Ads are shown to the visitors while they browse the web.
2. Remarketing lists for search Ads: Ads are shown to the visitors while they search for what they need.
3. Dynamic Remarketing: Visitors are shown dynamically created ads powered by your Google Merchant Centre Account. This is used to reach out to the advertisers and the ads are created on the basis of how customers visited the site and what pages were viewed.
4. Remarketing for mobile apps: Ads are shown to the visitors who used mobile apps to visit the site.

What is Remarketing List?

Remarketing list is the collection of cookies and tags from people who have visited the site. In order to run the remarketing campaign successfully, remarketing lists plays the most important role. It helps in knowing all the potential customers which should be reached and can be right target.

Remarketing list can be created by going to the "shared library" in AdWords.

Once remarketing lists is created it is added to the ad group. Ad Group can vary depending on the type of remarketing campaign.

Working:

The most important step while starting the remarketing campaign is adding the remarketing tag to the site. A tag is a small piece of code usually added to footer of the web page. Once the remarketing tag is added to the web page, remarketing lists are created. Remarketing lists are generally created for each web page depending on the category of product. For example: Remarketing list can be named as "Gadget list "for the web page containing electronic gadgets. So whenever a visitor visits this page, his cookie is added to the list so that he can be reached in future.

Remarketing campaigns needs to be designed in such a manner that they utilise the remarketing lists. Remarketing lists enables the business owners to reach out to the potential users with the ads related to the specific items that the customers were looking for.

Example: Suppose people looking for Sweaters visit the online store and checks out available items. These visitors can be added to a "Winter Wears" list, which would help in showing them ads related to winter wears. Then the ads related to winter wears can be shown to these visitors while they browse other websites.

Advantages of Remarketing:

- Personal and targeted advertising – No unnecessary impressions but precise targeting of users
- Name recognition increases

- Top of mind – Once the user has shown interest on the product and then showing the ad with same product will keep that product on top of his mind
- More conversion – Easy to get the user convert who has shown some interest
- Lower cost per conversion – By focusing to a very specific audience, you avoid irrelevant ads leading to a more efficient management of the budget

Disadvantages of Remarketing:

- High content Spam
- Overload banners
- No control over placement

Remarketing Strategies:

Remarketing in itself is not difficult. Good and efficient remarketing is an art. "The sky is the limit". Here the principle is to be creative with other words and does not focus just to people who have visited the site.

A few simple strategies:

- Visitors without a conversion: if you have a configurator application for a car brand, focus your remarketing campaign to people who have completed the full configurator yet no info brochure or appointment asked.
- Visit time: a visitor who has done your Christmas shop, a purchase can be re interested in a purchase for the Christmas period.
- Cross-selling: someone who has bought a printer may also be interested in printing paper and cartridges for this.

USES and BEST Practices for Remarketing:

- Usually people add items in their shopping cart but don't purchase them. So, remarketing lists can be created in such a way that helps in reaching out to users who visited the site and added the items in their shopping cart.

- Remarketing helps in reaching out to the customers when they are most likely to buy.
- Ads with special discounts on the items which the visitor is interested in, helps in pulling the customer back to the site.
- Large no. of users can be reached out, that too multiple times in a day.
- Ads can be shown only to those websites where they get better response, this would improve the performance of remarketing campaign.

Demographic Targeting

Definition:

Demographics can be defined as the parameters which are used in segmenting the targeted audience into more specific groups. Some commonly used demographics include gender, age, location, languages known, annual income, parental status etc. Depending on these traits audience is segmented into more specific groups which automatically makes a precise and accurate targeting

The use of demographic targeting can help the advertiser to target the right audience reducing the unnecessary impressions thus indirectly saving budget. The targeting is no more a tough zone as almost all the ad server provides such facility of doing demographic targeting. Knowing the business has no relation to kids it is always better to exclude users below 18 years old similarly if the product is related to female it is better to exclude male audience, etc.

The demographic variables are the most commonly used segmentation bases for the distinction of groups of customers and consumers. They are also the easiest to evaluate and helps in targeting the accurate users.

Demographic segmentation is so important that even when the market is not described in terms of population, it is necessary to relate the demographic characteristics so that one can estimate the size of the target market and the means of communication should be used to achieve it more efficiently.

Needs, desires, demands and consumption habits of customers are often related to these variables. Thus, the market is divided into groups of basic demographic variables such as social class, gender, age, family size, income generation.

Role of these demographics in Advertising World:

Advertisers use demographic traits like gender, age, location, languages known, annual income to group the audience in more specified groups. All members of the groups share the common trait. So, when the advertiser wants to run a campaign aimed at the specific group of people then that campaign is only served to the group that contains those traits at which the campaign is targeted.

Demographic segmentation enables advertisers to identify the potential audience for ads and product which are meant for the specific group of the population with common traits.

Advertisers are able to identify when and where the ad should be positioned so as to achieve maximum profits. Advertisers generally combine number of parameters to define the demographic profile.

Difference between Target Market and Demographic Targeting:

Although both the target market and demographic targeting belong to broader marketing segmentation process known as S-T-P marketing i.e. Segmentation, Targeting, and Positioning. But there is a slight difference between what these two are aimed at.

Target Market aims at advertisers identifying the potential market which could guarantee them better results and maximum profits. Few of the parameters which are taken into account while looking for the potential market are Market size, growth potential, number of competitors and company strengths.

Demographic targeting aims at segmenting the audience based on the shared traits and then targeting them with the campaign meant for them. Demographic segmentation works best when a product has customers with clearly definable personal traits.

For e.g.: Suppose a company has a product which is best for males aged between 18-25 yrs. and has an annual income of $ 50,000. So, the company would create a demographic group based on three parameters.

- Based on age.
- Based on gender
- Based on annual income

Among the demographic variables used for segmentation include (Detailed):

Age and Life Cycle

- The needs and choices in time consuming, vary with age and stage of life of consumers.
- This distinction can be made by dividing the market:

Age groups:

Majorly used demo targeting is age group as maximum advertiser targets the user as per their age, if the product is not related to child it is always excluded so that there is no unnecessary impression and budget burn. Similarly, they customize the targeting as per their target users. General category under age is made as below:

- Below 6 years;
- 6 to 11 years;
- 12 to 19 years;
- 20 to 34 years;
- 35 to 49 years;
- 50 to 64 years and
- Over 65 years.

Lifecycle Phases:

As an example of the segmentation stage in the life cycle, the market could be divided between:

- Children, youth, adults, and seniors;
- Singles and married;
- With or without children;
- By the age of the children still living in the parental home;
- For family size or the number of children who still live with their parents.

Sex:

Expectations and consumer preferences vary according to gender consumers. Companies are increasingly able to recognize these differences and provide options to meet the different requirements arising from this demographic variable. Products and services are designed with differentiated features to please both the male audience as the female audience. Categorization is always as below:

- Male
- Female
- Uncategorized

Yield:

This is one of the variables used, however, the income should not be considered in isolation, as there are other factors that determine the propensity to consume certain products and services. The division of the market held by the income variable usually considered a total income of families with values expressed in dollars and number of minimum wages. Categorization is general as below:

- Less than 9.999
- 10 thousand to 14,999
- Of 15-19999
- From 20,000 to 29,999
- From 30,000 to 49,999
- From 50,000 to 99,999, and
- Over 100 000.

Occupation:

Another category is based on the occupation of the user, at times, advertiser expects to target the user based on its occupation, for example if the advertiser is related to some kitchen stuff the then main targeted users they expect is the housewife who uses the internet. Categorization can be as below:

- Professionals and technicians
- Managers, entrepreneurs and public officials
- Clerks, salesmen
- Artisans
- Supervisors
- Operators

- Retirees
- Students
- Stay-at-home, and
- Unemployed

Social class:

Social class has a strong influence on consumer behavior. Many companies focus their activities on meeting specific social classes. However, it is important to remember that the preferences of social classes can change over time and there are several other important features to consider for market segmentation. Social classes can be distributed as Class A1; Class A2; Class B1; Class B2; Class C1; Class C2; Class D and Class E or generalized form as below:

- Low
- Low to high
- Medium to high
- Average
- Medium to high
- High, and
- High-high.

Generation

Each generation is influenced by the time it was created. Music, movies, fashion, political movements, events and ideologies of each period, influences the motivations and habits. A division currently much used distinguishes between the generations:

- Generation of the baby boomers – born between 1945 and 1964;
- Generation X – born from the early 1960s until the late 1970s, reaching the early 1980s, without exceeding 1984;
- Generation Y – also called Internet generation, born after 1980, according to some authors, also covers some born between the mid-1970s to mid-1990s.
- Generation Z – those born since the mid-1990s until the present day.

Not sure whom to target? Follow the below steps!

Here's the quick step-by-step list of creating and measuring an effective demographic campaign:

1. Run a demographic report to see what demographics are converting for you.
2. Create a new placement campaign where all the sites are ones where demographic bids apply (you don't have to choose every site that allows demographic bidding, however, since it's a demographic campaign, the placements you do choose should be part of that list).
3. Enable demographic bidding and bid based upon how different groups respond to your ads.
   Note: It can be helpful to set low bids and then use the demographic bidding options to raise them considerably. Since the demographic bidding options only allow you to raise bids (you can't bid less for a demographic), your placement bids should be what you're willing to pay for anyone, regardless of demographic characteristics to view your ad.
4. With placement campaigns, you bid at the placement level, not the keyword level, therefore, benchmark each placement campaign for performance for your initial bid, and then the demographic bidding 'bid booster' will raise your bids when the correct demographics view your ads.
5. Run both placement and demographic reports to see your conversion statistics.
6. Change your bids/placements as appropriate.

Behavioral Targeting

As the name says it targets the users as per their BEHAVIOR, if any user's behavior is categorized as sports enthusiast so showing him some sports related Ads will increase the probability of some response. Behavior targeting promises to target the right user as per the advertiser product, say an advertiser HP wants' to advertise their new product so targeting the users with Techi behavior will show more interest rather than users showing behavior for sports. This technique has helped a lot to increase the effectiveness of campaigns running for any product.

To define in one line: *Behavior targeting is a technique or ability to target users based on their behavior on the internet.*

The concept of Behavior targeting says – The ad shown to the user should not be relevant to the page but to the user. This technique was the great help to the marketers as now they can directly target the interested users only.

Behavior targeting is nothing but knowing each and every impression where to be served. It's about the knowing your customer well.

What made behavior targeting possible?

The one and the only thing which made this technique works is TRACKING technology. Collecting user's information made it possible to know about the behavior of the user. The tracking can be performed in multiple ways like if a customer registers with an e-commerce site to make a purchase, those sales along with the user's site navigation history are often stored and analysed to make targeted offers the next time the user comes online. Also even without registration, the site might place that information in a cookie, which is saved on the customer's hard disk and when the user revisits the site, the cookie is sent to the Web server making it easy to target the user. Above these all way, there is one deeper way to track data is for ISPs to perform deep packet inspection on their customer's traffic to determine the types of websites they visit and then the data are sold to marketing and ad serving companies to deliver more personalized ads which is we know very common these days. Many ad serving companies buy the behavior data from third party like exelate, dataLogix etc.

What is the exact information that is tracked?

- Page views
- Keywords
- Demographics information
- Content that is being read
- Sections on the site that is normally checked out by a user
- Searches made

- Domain
- Geographic location (IP)

What data is used to select the relevant of highly predictive anonymous visitor profile?

Behavior Variables:

- New/return visitor
- Previous visits to network
- Previous online purchases
- Previous campaign exposure
- Previous campaign response

Environment Variables:

- IP address
- Country of origin
- Time zone
- Operating system
- Browser type
- Screen resolution

Temporal Variables:

- Time of day
- Day of week
- Recency
- Frequency

Other Variables:

- Referring domain
- Search keywords

Types of Behavioral Targeting:

Behavior targeting has two major categorizations: one is which helps in targeting all users as per behavior for your website on the internet called as Network behavioral targeting and the other one which helps in targeting user within the website with different offers and promotions is called as Onsite behavior targeting.

1. Onsite Behavioral targeting:
   If the behavioral targeting is done solely on one particular website, that is targeting certain content based on the behavior or information of the visitor then its Onsite Behavioral Targeting. Onsite BT plays a significant role in relationship building and customer retention once they've arrived at your website. Onsite behavioral targeting enables you to customize your website to create the most welcoming, enticing destination for your each visitor and ultimately engaging them more deeply in your site thus expecting some good response. Example: You hold a shopping site, what if every visitor is treated in the same way? Naturally the user will lose the interest in time... Using onsite behavior targeting helps you to categorize your customer and the show relevant products, promotions, etc. which keeps up the interest of the visitor on the site to check more products. That's Onsite Behavioral targeting!

2. Network Behavioral targeting:
   Another type of behavior targeting is network behavior targeting which uses customer's or visitor's browsing history which reveals the information about who that person is – like marital status, sex, age range, interests, etc. to target the user with relevant advertising on different sites in internet. This kind of targeting is more famous and familiar to the marketers; this targeting is done through showing Advertisement on different publishers or sites. Most Ad networks use this kind of behavior targeting!

Working of Behavioral targeting:

Basically, behavioral targeting works through cookies on your browser. Each time you go to a website, they send cookies to your browser. These cookies then keep a log of the websites you have visited and try to develop an approximate personality. The surfing of internet forms a behavior of every user which is then used to target them as per their personality.

Let's know in steps how it starts to work:

Steps:

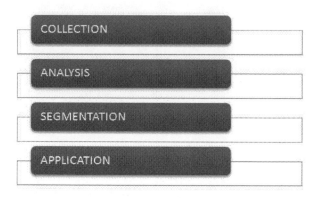

- STEP 1: Collection
  This step only deals with collecting users data, the data is collected as per cookies, searches etc.

- STEP 2: Analysis
  This step involves a lot of analysis on the data collected, the data collected is then checked if it's robot data or actual data. A different analysis is done on it.

- STEP 3: Segmentation
  After the data has been analysed and known what type of data we have received or collected it is then segmented into different segments as per behaviors, like the users showing the behavior as gadget freak will go into gadget segment, similarly the users showing behavior of aged person will go into the different segment. This way lot of segments are formed so as to target the users as per the product.

- STEP 4: Application
  Once we have the segmented data we are ready to apply it on campaigns as per the product/ advertiser. If the advertiser is of HP, we will be targeting behavior of Consumer electronics so as to catch up the users who fall into that segment increasing the probability of response.

Important points to be noted before applying BEHAVIOR TARGETING

1. Know deeper about your customer – More you know about your customer, easier it will be to make business and get best out of it.
2. Consider Ad content too – If the Ad content is matched up with the content on the page the ad needs to be shown will increase the probability of the user to show interest on the Ad.

Three main benefits from BEHAVIOR TARGETING are:

1. More Click-through
2. More Conversions
3. Improved ROI (return on investment)

Privacy Concerns:

Trust is always a concern in anything so when it's about behavior targeting it has to be as this technique uses the personal data. But behavioral targeting companies claim that they are highly responsible for these data, and impose the number of bans and regulations. But still some consumers are not that confident.

Contextual Targeting

Contextual meaning says" relating to or determined by or in context", so when it's about contextual advertising it means the Ads shown as per the content of the web page is contextual advertising. It is also a kind of targeted advertising in which Ads are always shown as per the contents present on a web page, e.g. if a user will be on a sports website he will be shown Ads related to sports, if in any entertainments site he will be shown Ads of movies, music, etc. Contextual advertising is also called "In-Text" advertising or "In-Context" technology, In-Text advertising has a small difference i.e. it works when a specific word or keywords within the text of a web page are matched with advertising and/or related information units.

To define in one go "Contextual targeting is a technique in which the web page is scanned to show the relevant Ad as per the content on the page".

Technically if you define "Contextual targeting is a technology which uses artificial intelligence to define and understand content rich websites and match them with targeted keywords so as to show up related Ad as per the content of the page"

The advertisements themselves are selected and served by automated systems based on the content displayed to the user. Contextual Advertising is in huge demand today as it brings good profit in return plus it's the latest online advertising technological advance and allows a company to place advertisements in major websites and portals that are carrying relevant content for their product or service which thereby bringing a good response.

"Just in a case, think as a user when you are searching for some property to buy and searching number of real estate's site and if some good property related Ads are shown to that user, there will be percentage of chance that user will show his interest on it as he is searching the related information only."

Categories:

We have a number of categories defined but as per IAB standards, the list can be of 23 top level categories and around 200 categories in total (including subcategories).

23 TOP Level Categories:

1. Arts & Entertainment
2. Automotive
3. Business
4. Careers
5. Education
6. Family & Parenting
7. Food & Drink
8. Health & Fitness
9. Hobbies & Interest
10. Home & Garden

11. Law, Government & Policies
12. News
13. Personal Finance
14. Pets
15. Real Estates
16. Religion & Spirituality
17. Science
18. Society
19. Shopping
20. Sports
21. Style & Fashion
22. Technology & Computing
23. Travel

How does Contextual Targeting work?

Contextual targeting generally works through a piece of code that you put on your web pages. The function of the code is to look through what is on the page and pull relevant ads from the company sponsoring the contextual targeting, which it then places on the site.

Contextual targeting is totally a dynamic approach. When a user requests a page, the page will have a JavaScript code embedded on it which will make a request to an Ad server with some Meta data information about the context of the page. This information could be the number of options like the URL of the page, the page content, or to be specific the section of the site where the user is... All these information are passed not as a text but as **keywords** (Keywords chosen plays the game in the working of contextual targeting) which will be more than enough for an Ad server to understand the context of the page but that highly depends on the Ad server potential. Every Ad server has its own targeting rules to be followed, for e.g. the keyword passed by the JavaScript say "sports" will co-relate with rule or condition set for sports category in the ad server and will then serve the content-specific ad from the ad server. Say an Ad Network is having a contextual targeting of sports channel for a particular product say a badminton racket and a publisher say ESPN sports has embedded a code (helps in contextual targeting) in his page to show ads related to its content. So whenever a user who shows interest on badminton page of ESPN site, automatically the ads related to the same context will be pulled up from the Ad Server to be shown on the page.

Advantage of Contextual Targeting:

- Greater engagement
- Higher conversion
- Content or Ads can be automatically matched to your content
- More benefit for publishers as higher chances of clicking on the Ad
- Relevant Ads as per the content don't annoy the user
- Saves unnecessary impressions

What is the difference between search engine optimization (SEO) and contextual advertising?

S. No.	Search Engine Optimization (SEO)	Contextual Advertising
1.	The purpose of SEO is to promote the site in search engine results for certain queries.	Contextual advertising is a form of advertising whose purpose is to promote or send relevant traffic to website
2.	The result is delayed in time	Instant results
3.	The effect of SEO is long term	The effect stops once the advertising campaigns stop
4.	SEO helps in organic traffic to the site	Contextual ads sends paid traffic to the site
5.	The number of visitors does not depend on the budget	The number of visitors depends on the budget, more the budget more is the visitors
6.	Changes take time	Changes done on the campaign are instant
7.	SEO does not guarantee of your top position for any keyword but assures in the increase of traffic	Contextual advertising gives guaranteed results

Geographic Targeting

Definition:

"The targeting of users as per zip code, area code, city, DMA, state, and/or country is called as geographic targeting". Geographic targeting is the practice of targeting ads to web users based on their physical location, e.g. If I want to show to ad only to US citizen I can target the Geo only to US so no other user at the different location can see the ad.

Geographic targeting is not a new concept but a very common criteria coming from the time when web advertising was not there, the other means of advertising which was there before web advertising was newspaper, radio stations, billboards, TV which was automatically Geo (local) targeted and also covered the around places but it's true not like the way it is targeted today.

The real Geographic targeting need came into need only when web advertising came into existence as generally all the publishers were global, now to make this possible a geolocation service was required, a geolocation service is a service which provides real-world geographic location of an object, such as a radar, mobile phone or an Internet-connected computer terminal.

Overview:

As we know Geographic targeting is the common criteria of every campaign in online advertising so all the ads to be served must have to pass this criterion before being rendered on a web page and this criterion is taken care by the ad server including all the other criteria's such as frequency capping, behavior targeting, end date, start date of campaign, impression goal, etc. All these checks are done by ad server and that too in milliseconds.

The process of selecting an ad by an ad server is called Ad selection or matching process, but this process does not satisfy in checking the Geographic targeting criteria as it runs for other features like ad size, impression goal, etc. The reason is clear as ad selection process works on pre-defined values given to an ad server but with Geographic targeting it is not possible as every time the ad server gets a request a query is made which then gives the result like country, state, and zip code. Etc. Let's know the proper working now.

WORKING: It's all about IP's!

In the real working of geographic targeting, it's the IP address which plays the game. As mentioned, there are no such pre-defined values set for geographic targeting criteria, it's always through queries the ad server gets the live value. Geographic targeting works on mapping process, it completely depends on mapping/connecting a USER's IP address with its physical location i.e. using the IP address of a user the location is tracked not exact but yes nearby like in which city, state or country depending upon our need. So now as we know IP address plays all the game in tracking there are the number of processes which are followed within to catch a single IP address after which the physical location is tracked.

The processes include: This all process comes under geo-location services!

- PINGS – Ping is a basic Internet program that allows a user to verify that a particular IP address exists and can accept requests.
- TRACEROUTE – Traceroute is a process of recording network routing process of the ping services i.e. it's a utility that records the route (the specific gateway computers at each hop) through the Internet between your computer and a specified destination computer. The routing of the ping can off-course lead to the last router which will send the information requested by the user and trace route plays the main role by giving the IP address of a final router which will surely be geographically near to user.
- REVERSE DNS - Reverse DNS is a method of resolving an IP address into a domain name, just as the DNS resolves domain names into associated IP addresses.

How the three processes helps Geo Location Services to catch the Physical Location?

The ISP (user's ISP) eventually moves the packet of information to a nearby network router to the user, which connects directly to the user. By using the trace route utility, the geolocation service can know every system the information was passed through in order to get to its final destination. The final important piece of information the service gets from a trace route process is the IP address of that final network router which will off-course be geographically nearest to the user, thus getting the around location of the user. Now when we have the network router's IP address in hand, the next process which is reverse DNS can be used to get the domain name or to identify who owns that network router which in than can be used to lock in on the physical location of the user. Example, if you are using an Airtel broadband connection, using this service you will get to know the region from where the request is coming which indirectly solves our purpose.

Limitations of Geolocation:

This service has improved a lot in its accuracy but still it's not always accurate and has some limitations like:

- If IP address is associated with the wrong location, everything goes wrong!
- If the address is associated with a very broad geographic location area then it's difficult to get the nearest location of the user.

Ad Server Role:

After the physical location has been tracked, the value passes to the ad server so that it renders right ad to the right user. There is again a mapping process followed to serve the right ad at the right location.

Step-wise process:

STEP 1:

Tracking of IP address using the above processes.

STEP 2:

Using the IP address the user physical location is tracked. (Explained above)

STEP 3:

Say the location of the user is Alabama (US)

STEP 4:

The location value is passed to ad server which then maps with its own Geo database (a database maintained but ad server internally, each location is given a unique value).

STEP 5:

MAPPING PROCESS – Say Alabama value stored in Ad server geo database is 22, the physical location value maps with the value of ad server database.

STEP 6:

The flights or ads targeted to Alabama shows up the ad to the user surfing from Alabama

In General geographical targeting could be done basis three forms of data:

1. *Technical targeting* basis latitude and longitude or basis IP address
2. *User-declared* information i.e. user has updated its current location
3. *Usage-based* i.e. this type of targeting is done for anonymous user whom the server targets basis the surfing behavior

AD VERIFICATION

Definition:

By IAB – "A process which attempts to verify that one or more attributes of a served online ad have been executed in a manner consistent with the terms specified by the advertiser or agency and agreed to as part of the ad campaign terms".

Ad verification is about checking the banner or the ad appearing at the right place i.e. right web page so that it can catch the right audience. It's the new area of digital marketing technology that has the potential to change how marketers buy media and how impressions are valued in the marketplace. It is truly beneficial for agency or advertiser to keep track of his online ad campaign giving clearer understanding of how ad campaign has performed, depending on which the further decision can be taken.

Ad verification ensures every impression as quality impression plus ensures it is served basis the targeting deal that was made by the advertiser or agency before starting the campaign. Ad verification companies reports all the validated and invalidated data, in fact multiple forms of data are reported by such technological companies which helps take a right decision for the successful campaign delivery.

Four primary areas that verification companies help the advertiser with, are:

1. Fraudulent traffic
2. Viewabilty
3. Geotargeting
4. Ad placement

With growing technology some companies have started to give more insights about the ad delivery but the basic areas remain the same as the above four are the most common that advertisers are always interested in.

Concern:

Nowadays it's the major issue that concerns both marketers and publishers for ensuring that ads appear on intended websites or pages and that they reach their targeted audiences. To help overcome this issue, companies began taking part in ad verification, typically utilizing third-party services to check their ads for any discrepancies that may be hindering optimal delivery. The Best known companies that offer ad verification technology are Double Verify, AdSafe Media, and AdXPose, etc. Such companies ensures brand safety by not letting the ad serve at wrong or irrelevant places.

Process:

Pictorial Explanation or Ad Verification process:

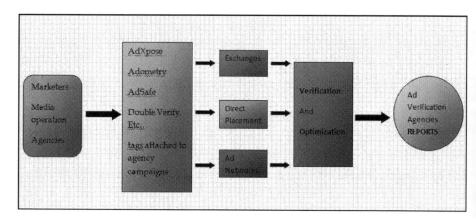

STEPS:

The marketers or Media reaches the Ad verification agencies for the It's Ads to be served securely at the right place.

The Ad verification agencies wrap the tags with their snippet, example if the creative is of DART, when wrapped by Adsafe it becomes "Dart tag wrapped with Adsafe".For your reference: Look at the code below:,

```
<SCRIPT language='JavaScript1.1' SRC="http://fw.adsafeprotected.
com/rjss/dc/xxxxx/xxxxx/adj/N258.the__nation/Bxxxxxxx.2;sz=728x90
;ord=[timestamp]?">
</SCRIPT>
<NOSCRIPT>
<A HREF="http://ad.doubleclick.net/jump/N258.the__nation/Bxxxxxxx
.2;sz=728x90;ord=[timestamp]?">
<IMG SRC="http://fw.adsafeprotected.com/rfw/dc/xxxxx/xxxxx/ad/N258.
the__nation/Bxxxxxxx.2;sz=728x90;ord=[timestamp]?"
BORDER=0 WIDTH=728 HEIGHT=90 ALT="Advertisement"></A>
</NOSCRIPT>
```

*This is a Dart tag wrapped with Adsafe.

Now the wrapped up tags are sent to the Ad Networks, Exchanges or Direct Placement to traffic and make the Ads live and there after the Ad verification vendor works starts. At the end, they provide with the reports having performance data, placement, and engagements etc. using which further optimization is done.

One big reason for all these verification processes is due to JavaScript not being a secure language. Any script in a page has intimate access to all of the information and relationships of the page. This makes use of mashups and scripted advertising unacceptably risky, so raising the need of Ad verification companies who takes care of this risk by their own respective procedures.

Advantages:

- Helps in better ROI
- Proper track of the campaign
- Data dependent decisions which helps in taking right decision on the campaign
- Optimization process goes in ease as ad verification data helps in saving time with some insightful data
- Media team, with the help of past data negotiate on their future media buys
- Ensures brand safety
- Saves advertisers budget by invalidating unwanted impressions

Difference between Ad Verification and Ad Validation:

S No.	AD VERIFICATION	AD VALIDATION
1.	Ad verification is the process of checking the banner or the Ad is appearing at the right place i.e. right web page so that it can catch the right audience	Ad Validation is a tool/process that provides automatic validation (quality assurance) of online ads for publishers, advertisers, agencies and ad networks.
2.	In simple words, ad verification is verifying of ads before it renders on a page.	Ads validation is a check on the number of features of an ad so that it does not create any problem for publishers (mainly), advertisers, and agencies too.
3.	It automates the QA process of checking the ads appearing on intended websites	It automate the QA process of checking the ad tags
4.	This process save the wastage of impressions	This process saves time in checking the ads
5.	Ads are not checked internally	Technical aspects of ads are checked like CPU usage, click tag format, frame rate, flash version, etc.
6.	It's the best technology when the ads have to spread across hundreds or even thousands of sites.	It's the best technology when there are number of ads to check, saves too much of manual work
7.	Geographic check	They work irrespective of location

Some well-known companies that provide ad verification services are:

- Adometry
- DoubleVerify
- Project Sunblock
- IAS
- Adledge
- GeoEdge
- The Media Trust

- Proximic
- AdSafe Media
- Peer39
- RocketFuel
- AdXpose
- Performline
- Telemetry

AD VIEWABILITY

The only objective of serving the ads online is to make them available to the customers. An ad is of no use if it's not visible to the users. So, mere serving an ad is not enough for successful campaign, we need to ensure that it's being viewed by the customers.

Definition:

Ad Viewability can be defined as the online advertising metric which keeps the track of those impressions which are actually viewed by the customers.

What is a viewable impression?

A served ad impressions becomes a viewable impressions if its contents are available in viewable space of the browser window, on an in-focus browser tab, fulfilling the basic criteria for an ad to be considered viewable such as the percent of ad pixels within the viewable space and the length of time the ad is in the viewable space of the browser.

For example, if an ad is loaded in the bottom of a web page, but a user does not scroll to view, that would not be considered visible.

Why Ad viewability concept did come into existence?

To every new thing there is always a need behind, similarly ad viewability came into existence due to advertiser started to complain and expected proof about their ad being viewed to the targeted users. The only solution was to calculate or measure the viewability of ad being rendered on the web page thus such new emergence.

The IAB reported that 54% of all online advertising is not seen by users and this was concluded looking at many factors like:

- Many times the ad is loaded out of sight of the user, since user does not scroll the page
- The ad does not load in time due to slow bandwidth or network issues
- The announcement has plugins that the user does not have
- Due to use Ad blockers by users

Thus advertisers getting educated about such factors made them realize to pay only for viewable ads and not just served impressions thus leading to new metric called CPMV i.e. cost per mille viewable ads.

Google, one of the giants of the advertising network, announced in December 2013 that they will only charge for ads viewed. To define what is considered ad seen and what not, Google has worked directly with the Media Rating Council using the standard proposed by the Interactive Advertising Bureau.

When is an Impression considered to be viewable impression?

Let's know the requirement for an impression to be considered as Viewable Impression:

1. Pixel Requirement: Minimum 50% pixels of the ad must be visible in viewable space of the browser.
2. Time Requirement: The ad must be visible in browser for minimum time of one continuous second, post ad render.

Both these requirements must be determined in a specific order. Only once the pixel requirement is fulfilled, then we can determine the time requirement.

Some other requirements or criteria to determine the viewable impressions are:

- User Actions:
  If it is determined that the user is actively interacting with the ad such as clicking on the ad then this can be considered as viewable impression even if it doesn't meet the pixel and time criteria. A mere mouse-over would not be considered as viewable impressions. A user must indulge on a call for action for the impression to be considered as viewable.

- Determining Viewability through ad and ad Container:
  Viewability is usually measured by the ad, through the JavaScript tag attached to the ad. But sometimes this tag is not attached to the Ad. So, in those cases, viewability can be measured through the Ad container in which the Ad appears. Determining Viewability on the basis of the ad container involves an inference that the ad, in fact, appeared within the container in its intended format. Usually, measurement based on ad is preferred, but in scenarios where this can't be applied, Ad Container measurement is accepted.

- Large Display Ads:
  Large Ads usually occupy more space on the browser, so fulfilling pixel criteria of 50% would not be feasible for it. So, for large display ads if 30% pixels of the ad lies in the viewable space of the browser for a minimum of one second then it's considered as Viewable Impression.

- Expandable Rich Media Ads:
  There are certain ads which normally appears in the browser in small size, and once the user interacts with it, they expand. For these ads, viewability can be measured in two ways. Either we can measure the pixel count when the ad is in initial small size or we can examine the pixel once the ad expands. If we are considering pixel count for an ad in initial size then time requirement should be examined for both pre-expansion and expanded the state. But, if we are considering pixel count for expanded ad then time requirement is also counted for an expanded ad.

Benefit of Ad Viewability:

Advertisers usually pay for each impression which is served irrespective of whether it's being viewed by the customers or not and due to which advertisers has to bear a loss of several dollars. Realizing the loss, the advertisers wanted to shift from impression served standard to impression viewed standard.

Ad Viewability concept in USA

In the US, the advertising industry is already a step ahead in regards to the use of ad viewability technology. Advertisers are no more reluctant about paying extra bucks for ad viewability as they are well educated about the pros and cons of the same. This also makes you realize of the fact that viewability is becoming the new currency in online advertising. There are advertisers who has accepted this extra spends as their part of advertising funds and include the viewability objective as their one of the goal.

There are countries who are not much aware of ad viewability and if they are aware of it, they are reluctant spending on it. The technology is spreading and in coming time it will become an objective for almost all the advertisers.

To Conclude:

Ad viewability represents a significant change in the way online media in the sale and tracking cookies and improves allocation models, making them more accurate.

It is proven that greater ad viewability, improves the performance of the brand and direct response campaign but we will still have to wait for it to be more universal to know it's all over the impact on the online advertising market.

AD OPERATION TOOLS

What are Ad Operation tools?

Ad operation tools are the software that is used before taking the campaign live, these tools are basically the utility tools involved in the successful execution of online ads or online campaign. These tools are used by the ad operation teams who are responsible for making the campaign live i.e. making the ads live on the internet.

The Ad Operation requires a number of checking and inspection as it's the key team in an online advertising industry. Any small mistake can hamper the whole campaign and ultimately loss of the client. E.g. Improper implementation of click Tag, impression tracker or any 1×1 pixel may lead to the huge discrepancy and as a result loss. Therefore the campaign implementation has to be checked properly before taking the campaign live.

With concentration and delicacy, we have some free tools available which ease the work of Adops and also conforming the right setup of a campaign. Let's know the common ones used all over the globe:

- Flash Validator
- HTTP FOX
- UAE
- FIDDLER
- ClickTag / Malware checker in Flash (Online)
- GHOSTERY
- FIREBUG
- FIRECOOKIE

- SOTHINK WEB VIDEO DOWNLOADER
- GEO EDGE PROXY TOOLBAR
- CHARLES
- SERVICE CAPTURE
- RichFLV
- YSlow
- Online Cookie Remover

Flash Validator:

It is well-known online tool that help you to validate your flash file. This tool by Google is available free where you need to upload your swf file to see if it's working fine before uploading it to campaign while trafficking. This is a quick way to QA your ad and confirm the client if it's working fine or not. It gives below information about the flash file:

- Flash Version
- File size
- Dimension
- Frame per second
- Compression
- Frames
- ClickTag: It assures if the flash file has the clickTag implemented, if not is gives the error message when clicked on the banner previewed after uploaded.

HttpFox:

The most used tool for debugging in online advertising by almost all the technical teams in online advertising. Ad Operation department make maximum use of this tool. This tool being so easy and user friendly helps in resolving the issue easily and catching the error if any before making any campaign live. HTTP fox is just an add-on for Mozilla which is very easy to install. This helps in checking all the pixel firing, all the tracking pixels like conversion, imprint, event pixels etc.

Technically it is the tool that monitors and analyses all incoming and outgoing HTTP traffic between the browser and the web servers.

UAE: (URL ACTION EDITOR)

UAE is a Windows application that lets you edit parameters of action scripts in Flash (SWF) files. UAE also has many other features like replacing symbols, editing linkage IDs, frame labels, importing new symbols and placing them on any timeline, editing location of symbols on any timeline etc.

UAE is an amazing tool to check the flash files easily, It's useful in checking the click Tag, background color, other variables (if defined) the version of flash and all the information related to the flash file.

It is very simple to use, just drag and drop the flash file which has to be checked, the tool will show all the information.

Fiddler:

It's an another interesting tool that is normally used, It helps in capturing the HTTP traffic issue if any. It's a Web Debugging Proxy which logs all HTTP(S) traffic between your computer and the Internet. It allows you to inspect traffic, set breakpoints, and "fiddle" with incoming or outgoing data. Fiddler includes a powerful event-based scripting subsystem, and can be extended using any .NET language.

ClickTag / Malware checker in Flash (Online):

We also have an online tool which helps in checking the flash file without any effort, we just need to upload the flash file and have to click to scan which will give us the complete report about the content, version, dimensions, weight, list of getURL and action scripts, detect security hole and malware presence.

Ghostery:

Tracking is often invisible, tools like these Firefox add-on aim to provide users with insight into the trackers they encounter on the web. It's a best tool (extension) which tells about the third party tracking, widgets or web bugs embedded on the visited site. We can make use of this tool in live plus while trafficking the cases at back end too, like we can save time by checking impression tracker firing without using HTTPFOX. E.g. if the tracker provided is of DoubleClick, when you open the specific ad it will shows written DoubleClick at the right upper corner.

Firebug:

Firebug is a web development tool that facilitates the debugging, editing, and monitoring of any type of website's HTML, JavaScript, asp, etc. Firebug is a fabulous tool but we will be only knowing this tool from Adops view and how helpful it can be.

Firebug is a free source plus it's an extension to Mozilla browser which can be easily downloaded and used. If you look from Adops point of view, it's the best tool to sort out ad serving errors, when things go wrong, Firebug lets you know immediately and gives you detailed and useful information about errors in JavaScript, CSS, and XML.

Firecookie:

It's a part of firebug now and is the best extension to view and manage cookies in your browser. The function this extension can perform are:

- You can inspect the cookie very well and can also see the values.
- Cookie permission for a specific website can be changed using this tool.
- Cookie expiration time can also be shown.
- The best part you can export all the cookies for the visited site on a text file.
- You can see both sent and relieved cookie. etc.

Sothink Web Video Downloader:

There are times when you require checking any live video ads, you can make use of this tool to download the video and inspect it for any errors or inspection. It is very easy to use, it is just an extension to Mozilla and whenever any video will be shown on the browser it will start to blink, stating that this can be downloaded.

GeoEdge Proxy Toolbar:

This tool is used to set any location worldwide to see the display of the web page or the display of the Ad on a web page from that location. The user sitting in UK can see how the Ad will appear for users sitting in other countries on a web page. It's a great and easy to use proxy tool. The content shown will be exactly the same that will be seen by other countries users, e.g. sitting in India if we select Arabic geo we will be shown the same context as will be seen by the Arabs (Arabic language).It's very useful for geo targeted Ads. As you can see the Ad appearance for US users.

Charles:

A Web debugging tool which shows you exactly what traffic is sent and received. It basically acts as a middle ware between the user (browser) and internet (web applications). With Charles you can quickly diagnose and rectify any problems you may be experiencing with your websites. Charles also provides bandwidth throttling, which allows you to experience websites as a modem user and can easily run at low speed. Charles also has a feature of rewrite URLs which sometime can be very beneficial. Great search function. You can also quickly download the content and as it a java based it runs on windows/mac/Linux. All together it's a great tool. Try and know it better.

Service Capture:

Another tool that can be very helpful in ad operation is service capture. This tool runs on your computer (PC or mac) and captures all HTTP traffic sent from your browser or IDE. It is designed to help Rich Internet Application (RIA) developers in the debugging, analysis, and testing of their applications.

Features:

- Remote Service Deserialization
- Bandwidth Simulation*URL to File Mapping
- Unit Testing
- Flash Trace Logging
- Monitor ANY Log File

RichFLV:

RichFLV is a tool used for video ads where FLV Medias are used. It's a tool where we can check the video files plus if required, we can edit them too.

Features:

- Read FLV Metadata
- read/edit/modify/delete cue points
- cut FLVs
- convert the sound of the FLV to mp3
- convert FLV to SWF

YSlow:

YSlow is a tool developed by Yahoo Engineers to analyses web pages and tells why they may be slow and suggests ways to improve their performance based on a set of rules for high-performance web pages. It is available with the firebug web development tool.

Features:

- It offers suggestions for improving the page's performance.
- Best and easy way to find out the reason for slowdowns in your website
- It grades web pages which make it simple
- Summarizes the web page's components
- Statistics display

Online Cookie Remover:

It's quick online tool that helps to remove the cookies from your browser. This is quite helpful during the QA of ads in ad operations. As multiple of times the ad that you are trying to look is not appearing after it has appeared once, the reason is frequency cap of 1 applied to the ad or the ad may appear just once to a user. So to have a look at the ad again, we need to clear the cookies. The online feature to remove cookies is provided by adobe. Click on the below URL and click "delete all sites" or the one that you want to delete just select and click the button saying "delete website".

HTML 5

Definition:

HTML means Hyper Text Markup Language. It is a set of rules that tell computers how to interpret code to display websites. In other words, HTML is how two computers speak to each other over the internet.

HTML attempted a lot of version with the first one in 1995 known as HTML 3.0 after then made way to a more practical plus logical approach known as HTML 3.2 which got completed in 1997. The same year another version was launch which was HTML 4 having a lot of more benefits then HTML 3.2.

The latest which has brought a lot of change and advancement is HTML5 which is the fifth version of these rules. It was launched in 2012 but is still in development, working on new additional features. HTML 5 brings a lot of changes especially the <canvas> element which killed the flash usage. It merges several technologies like video, audio, canvas & other design features) currently used to make websites interactive. HTML5 introduces a bunch of new features, including:

- Web applications that work when you are not connected to the internet.
- Drag and drop file uploads.
- Voice input.
- In it we don't required proprietary plugins n APIs like older versions of standard.
- It provides one common interface to make loading elements easier. Like while using it we don't need to install a flash plugin in HTML5 because the element will run by itself.

- It will reduce operational costs.
- Improve ad effectiveness.
- Offline editing is possible
- Common standard for storing data in databases

Other Major benefits of HTML5:

- Mutuality:
  With the help of HTML5 it is possible to embed video and audio, high-quality drawings, charts and animation and many other rich contents without using any plugins and third party programs as the functionality is built into the browser.

- Improved Semantics:
  HTML5 can increase the semantic value of the web page as the codes are very standardized. In other words, with the help of HTML5, it's easy to see which parts of the page are headers, footers, aside, etc. and most importantly their meaning and purpose in the whole format.

- Consistency:
  It helps to code a web page on one site compared to another. This will make it easier for designers and developers to immediately understand how a web page is structured as they can code a web page on one site compared to another.

- Improved Accessibility:
  After seeing the HTML5 elements of the page we can immediately make more detailed understanding of the structure of the page.

- Many new features & standards have emerged as a part of HTML5. Once you detect the available features in today's browsers, you can take advantage of those features in your application. Its main focus is to make easier application with easy front-ends, drags & drop tools, discussion boards & other useful elements.

- While building the site, the developer can specify the files that the browser should cache. So, even if you refresh the page when you are offline, the page will still load correctly. This sort of caching has several advantages like offline browsing, faster loading of files and reduced load on server.

• Database: Cookies have been used to track unique user data for years and the entire cookie data is added to every HTTP request header. This can end up having a measurable impact on response time. With HTML5, we can do better by using 2 types of storage - session storage & local storage in place of cookies. It's not a permanent database but enables you to store structured data temporarily.

Disadvantages or Challenges:

• Data Protection:
There is a certain vulnerability of HTML5 in the field of data protection compared to the standard HTML 4. If the HTML5 storage remains on the user's computer for many months, the websites, referring to it via JavaScript after the page loads, can be transparent to the user to collect and transmit data to the site owner. Having HTML 5 storage in the computer can obviously be more dangerous as user's hard drive can consist of a lot of personal data which can cause him heavy loss also.

• Multimedia compatibility:
A lot of functionality is still not responding perfectly as stated, e.g. full screen mode in video, playback, etc.

• Games development:
Shortcomings regarding the use of HTML5 to create games, due to which game developers are facing a lot of difficulties.

• Not supported by all older browsers:
More recently, not all browsers can work with HTML5 as all the new standard is not yet supported or compatible by now.

HTML 5 VS Flash:

1. Size:
   HTML5 Ads are measured as file size in whole including the backup images, click tags/codes and other including files whereas Flash ads weight limit is based on the creative size only. Thus, HTML5 ads are heavy in size and can be around 100Kb +.

2. Optimization:
   Flash automatically provides optimization for codes/assets and compiles everything into a single file which is already compact with the minimal number of files. For HTML5, no optimization tools are available yet. Thus, special attention shall be given on how HTML5 ads are packaged and delivered as it helps in quick ad load time.

3. Parent company:
   Flash is not an open standard, it is controlled by ADOBE systems whereas HTML5 is largely controlled by a committee managed by – MOZILLA, OPERA SOFTWARE and APPLE.

4. Cost:
   Constructing flash websites using adobe tools is expensive than HTML5. Making a website using HTML5 may require a lot of LOCs but is not expensive as flash websites

5. Convenience:
   HTML5 can render multimedia content easily without the necessity of installing a plugin or player application, unlike FLASH. Though HTML5 does have a downside to this, namely the fact that older browsers don't render it correctly or don't render it at all.

6. Picture Clarity:
   Flash has the ability to specify measures in subpixel which results in crisp and more pleasant appearance whereas HTML5 can lead to inconsistency and unreliability in display.

7. Mobile:

   Most important feature of HTML5 is its capability to run flexibly on Mobile because of which it's getting preference above FLASH as Flash is bound to PC only. The same ad unit can be used across devices.

8. Development:

   Flash has a larger resource pool and even larger community whereas HTML5 is fairly new technology so its compatibilities are quite limited.

9. Usability:

   Amount of processing power required to run HTML5 is considerably lower than Flash given the fact that more number of people are using mobile devices. Designers are also aiming to create different versions of websites for PC and mobile (Stripped down version).

10. Semantic Elements in HTML5 is the use of HTML mark-up to reinforce the semantic/meaning of the information in web pages and web applications rather than merely to define its presentation or look which can't be done via non-semantic elements i.e. <div>, <span>, etc. This helps in processing faster as the browser gets to know the purpose by the element whereas no such functionality in flash.

PROGRAMMATIC BUYING

Definition:

Programmatic media buying involves computer algorithms that allow quick purchase of ad impressions according to present parameters. It is an application of artificial intelligence which ensures that bid can be placed for advertising inventory in real time there by helping advertisers to get the desired ad space easily and cheaply.

Programmatic Buying refers to the process of purchasing digital advertising with the use of automated software's. The software like DSP, SSP, and Ad Exchange helps to automate the process as opposed to traditional process of buying and selling which involved manual human negotiations.

Introduction:

The programmatic development was born purchasing real-time spaces. Like the finance sector with its stock markets, trading online advertising has dematerialized. Buyers and sellers are now operating through automated platforms, invented in the United States and named ad exchanges. The fully automated concept allows achieving real-time audience through precise algorithms stirring all kinds of socio, demographic, behavioral and geographic data. The use of this technology extends to other screens (mobile phone and tablet) and gradually exceeds its primary objective to improve the performance of banners and video ads (display) on websites and to be interested in the forms of qualitative advertising communication (image campaign) as native advertising (numerical variation of the infomercial). The programmatic therefore reinvents business practices between advertisers and media, by inviting engineers, developers IT specialists and data mining (data scientist, chief data officer) to trade advertising space.

The RTB is a form of automation of transactions that allows programmatic buying. The first platforms launched by US Internet giant, DoubleClick Ad exchange from Google, Microsoft Advertising Exchange, Yahoo Ad Exchange, etc.

Programmatic offers unprecedented optimization of purchasing space on the digital canals. To an audience that disperses from one medium to another and follower of multiple screens at once (multi-tasking), the purpose of an advertising campaign is no longer limited to target specific target consumers without power, in addition, to truly assess efficiency. The programmatic,(the marketing automation space) is the answer to technology for better performance of advertising investments on the internet used from the marketing of low audience spaces or that of unsold ad exchanges have proved effective and rapidly entrusted with the sale of said premium gaps. In a split second, the programmatic real time permits addressing the right message at the right time to the right person.

Programmatic is set to spread to the entire market for the purchase of advertising spaces. Through targeting a hitherto unprecedented accuracy and greater efficiency, the programmatic is the promise to advertisers for best ROI (return on investment). If the algorithms have not replaced human labour advice and recommendations, tasks within media agencies are increasingly techniques. The programmatic attracted all the major advertisers; some devote already 20% of their advertising budget. In the short term, with the digitization of all media, it is just the market for the purchase of spaces - television, radio, and even display - which would be entrusted to electronic platforms to program real-time message delivery

The development of the connected TV and the rise of big data promises a bright future in programmatic. More efficient, algorithms now govern all the information activities and online communication. These mathematical formulas results to increasingly sophisticated and affect the supply and demand for content, whatever they are, and grow to digital conversion of the media industry professions. In addition, their omnipresence is not without asking the fundamental question of data protection

The advertising market due to Programmatic should see an annual growth rate of 50% by 2017.

Why Use Programmatic Buying?

The reason behind programmatic buying being widely accepted in advertising world is its capability to increase the effectiveness of the campaign. It helps to achieve improved results as campaign can target the potential audience.

Before programmatic buying, ad inventory was bought and sold through human negotiations which often took more time and was not reliable. With programmatic buying, the use of automated software ensures that no more human intervention is required in the process and also it's more efficient and cheap. But this doesn't mean that there is no need for humans, humans are definitely required for planning strategies about campaign management. The use of this automated software ensures that humans can now devote more time towards making better management programs which would help in running the campaign in the best possible manner.

How it works?

The data is the key element that drives the purchase program. For best results, buyers should enter as much information as possible about the target audience. Normally manufacturers have extensive data on their customers and can enter them to buy programmatic platform they choose to use. In addition, through the platform, brands can be purchased for further CPM data collected by third parties. Data provided by third parties may be demographic (e.g., Sex, age, annual income, etc...), Psychographic (attitudes and interests) and behavioral (recent searches, use of credit cards, etc...). Shopping platform program takes all this data and use to implement the campaign. The goal is not only to combine the right ad to the right customer but also deliver the ads to the right context, particularly in the context that leads to the fulfilment of the objective of the campaign.

As with search marketing, deals for the desired impressions are made and the platform is responsible for carrying out the purchase with an auction system that determines who gets which ads in milliseconds: this process is called Real Time Bidding (RTB). When it comes to buying digital media advertising programmatically, there are two main approaches used.

1. Based on the price (**price-based trading**), one tries to buy ads for the lowest possible price and seeks to benefit the campaign to try to reduce the cost as much as possible. It can be performed targeting the target audience and optimize this approach, which in practice tends to be rather manual and not automated.

2. The other approach is used with the purchase program and is based on the values (**value-based trading**). In this approach the system continually learns from ad responses and values each impressions. It is this value which helps the system to prioritise the most valued impressions against the higher bid and inexpensive impression against lower bid. By this way

Programmatic buying Options:

Programmatic provides three kinds of buying options for buyers to work on, below are the options:

Open Exchange or Market:

This is the most used out of three buying options. It has the largest inventory database on a low cost but the quality may differ as inventory validation is a challenge. Advertisers just need to get approved by the exchange to run on the open inventory. Open market is preferably recommended in the case higher reach or when the campaign is performance focused. Both buyer and seller participate in the open auction via RTB (Real Time Bidding) which eliminates the need to work directly with publishers or ad networks and negotiate on the pricing. In this buying model, the transparency comes with three options which also impacts on the inventory quality. The three options consists of below:

3. Fully Transparent
4. Semi Transparent
5. Blind

The above three name itself suggests what level of transparency each provides like in fully transparent the buyer can optimize at domain level whereas in semi, optimization is not possible at each domain level and the domains are masked with a single URL which hides the domain name from buyer, thereby helping buyer to optimize but not basis the actual domain URL. The last one which is blind where the buyer does not get any source information basis optimization can be done.

Private Market:

This is just opposite to open market as the inventory is private and not open to all advertisers but the publisher does have to invite advertisers to bid on their inventory whereas here the advertisers are approved by publishers and not exchanges. In this publishers offer specific pools of inventory which advertiser can target as per requirement. This buying option is much more convenient and easy to manage as post optimization buyers can transact against specific placements and spend money which is not possible in open market options. Private market can be well utilized for campaigns with focus as performance, brand or specific reach. Just because the targeting or control option is also in the hand of buyer transparency is well maintained whereas validation is easily possible.

Direct:

Direct option is chosen when the ad has to run on the specific publisher like Yahoo, MSN, etc. It's a non-auction based approach and guarantees on the direct buy with a lesser cost then the manual process of buying direct ad slots which also takes its own time. This option clearly helps in improving transactional efficiency and ability to access highly targeted placements in an automated manner. Cross-device targeting is possible with the feasibility of behavior/profile targeting also. Buyer opts for this option majorly in the case of branding as it helps in buying the premium inventory on a fixed cost with full transparency and high visibility of course.

Advantages of Programmatic Buying:

- Cost Effective – We have user data beforehand which helps in purchasing each impression as per targeting required and this saves a lot of unnecessary impressions. Though the impression served are based out of data the chances of conversion or required outcome is more thereby affecting the ROI positively.

- The programmatic purchase creates value, efficiency and performance for advertising market
- Better targeting of consumers – Programmatic buying enables advertisers to target the right audience in the right environment.
- Transparency – Transparency on the inventory bought provides additional reassurance to advertisers that their brand equity is preserved.
- Better monitoring of campaigns – You can always run your campaign as per your need, easily adjusted as per plan
- Quick Catch – Programmatic buying helps connect advertisers with audiences faster and smarter, on any device and on any channel in milliseconds.
- Enhancing the value of content
- Advertisers benefit from the improved performance of their campaigns and higher their productivities
- Efficient buying platform – Real fact of programmatic is that it has reduced a lot of manual approaches and also have cut down the unnecessary middlemen from the ad buying process. Unnecessary negotiation on pricing, positioning is no more a part of programmatic buying which saves a lot of time and yes money too.
- The rapid expansion of programmatic have led to better organize the practices of digital sector without making any compromise on the imperative transparency, responsible regulation is possible for the benefit of all market players and the future of this burgeoning sector
- Inventories are becoming more and more qualitative – To every best thing it takes time so did programmatic took, but now it's functioning full-fledged. Initially, publishers or advertisers were reluctant at first but slowly they started to invest with smaller budget and now they can see benefits out of it, similarity publishers see better earning and have started to participate more via RTB thereby leading to qualitative inventories for advertisers.
- For publishers, the programmatic is a real opportunity, sometimes a salvation – Some publishers quickly understood the interest of programmatic effect to promote their inventories and came together

to create large marketplaces and achieve critical mass and some still needs to be educated about its potential which we all are sure soon will happen. The effectiveness of RTB campaigns allowed publishers to revalue digital advertising. The display average CPM increased by a good percentage than before leading to much more earning than before and is supposed to go higher in coming times

- Programmatic performance is recognized by advertisers – The programmatic purchase allows advertisers to better target their prospects or customers. Indeed, the algorithms are becoming increasingly fast and pointing the integrating data sets – first-party or third party – is increasingly important. The technology has gone far better, today companies collect the user data beforehand by using their predictive model thus enabling precise or accurate targeting. The Leads captured are more qualified, the conversion is coming at lower cost than traditional purchase basically helping advertiser in better ROI which makes them more satisfied

- Helps to grow business at a rapid rate.

- Marketers can reach out to greater audience that too almost immediately.

- Results can be measured quickly and efficiently.

- Advertisers can reach out to right audience at the right time.

- Streamlined process helps in effective delivery of campaign to the targeted audience.

- Enable advertisers to purchase ad inventory one impression at a time thereby making it cost effective.

- With increased level of transparency in the business process, the advertisers and publishers can achieve greater level of confidence and trust among themselves.

Misconception about programmatic buying:

There is a misconception that Programmatic buying is same as Real time bidding but actually RTB is just a type of programmatic buying. Apart from RTB, programmatic buying also contains non-RTB processes like direct buying. We will cover RTB in detail in our next chapter.

Common Examples of Programmatic buying:

- Buying and Selling Ad Inventory using RTB and Ad Exchange.
- Direct Buying ad impressions from Publishers.
- Using Retargeting for campaign.

Expectation for Programmatic Growth:

Two major points that can lead to rapid growth are:

1. Development of all creative and technological ecosystems:
    Advertisers are now awaiting creative and technological solutions in a programmatic purchase. Now, creative agencies are increasingly integrating technology into their reasoning. Reconciliation between media agencies and creative agencies will lead to better business via programmatic which has started to happen quite often in the digital domain now. Thus, the trend is likely to accelerate to meet needs of advertisers soon.

2. Progressive learning of technologies is necessary in programmatic:
    The use of programmatic purchase requires adaptation, both from agencies and advertisers. For agency it is important so that they can explain the advertiser the real use of programmatic and its technology. The advertiser also has to realize and educate themselves and should start developing a skilful DMP whereas should also start using those data for targeted advertising. A better understanding the operation of these campaigns allow advertisers to better understand the marketing costs.

Major Concern:

The main issue of the regulation of programmatic is to promote the development of this sector -

Regulation should encourage the development of this sector - the offline sector is experiencing a marked slowdown in recent years, the growth of the online segment is brought in 2013 by the sharp increase in advertising spending in the programmatic. Today, we see the same and with this rapid increase soon digital will take a major part of revenue

Success for Programmatic Buying:

Sharp growth for Programmatic can be seen if the transparency is well maintained i.e. Transparency must be the central goal of the regulation of the programmatic market

- Transparency in the use of personal data
- Transparency in content purchases
- Transparency in financial flows

Above are the major points where transparency should be maintained so that advertisers are not hesitant in investing and yes a flexible and responsible regulation of this sector is required and desired by all stakeholders to make it a big success.

REAL TIME BIDDING

Let's go through the important topic i.e. RTB that is being discussed too much in Online advertising nowadays and is an actual fact as RTB is a reality that is changing the way online advertising is purchased.

What is RTB (Real Time Bidding)?

To so many RTB sounds so complex but it's nothing but a myth and is a technology that makes life easier for players of advertising: advertisers, publishers, advertising agencies, boards.

Definition:

Real time bidding is an automated process that enables buying and selling digital advertising inventory in real time. Advertisers bid on each impression and if the bid is won the ad is displayed on the publisher's site. The traditional method of display advertising involved manual negotiation where the brokers played a vital role in deciding the prices of inventory to be sold. In RTB the role of brokers is taken care by SSP and DSP.

The concept of RTB or real-time bidding was first popularized by Google in the development of AdWords where they pointed to the fact of buying auction keywords based targeted queries.

This technique is now widely used in the field of ad exchanges and shall mean the buy and sell display advertising space to bids based formats, targeting criteria and predefined budgets.

It covers two key concepts:

1. "Real-time" purchasing is done in real time, usually in less than 150 ms
2. "Bidding" is purchase advertising auction, which has a large impact on the ROI.

Why RTB?

Best answer to this will be through showing the drawbacks of traditional display advertising from the eyes of advertiser and publisher both:

For Advertisers, the traditional online display advertising lacked efficiency as most of the impressions had to be purchased at same price per unit, irrespective of their value to the campaign. Due to this even for impressions which had less impact on the campaign more price had to be paid.

For Publishers, the traditional advertising resulted in more than half of the inventory left unsold or if sold it was done for very low price.

It's a great help to both advertiser and publisher and so getting more famous and well known technology.

RTB working in brief:

The process starts as soon as the consumer browses through the publisher's website.

What actually happens is the ad space in publisher's inventory is sent across through SSP to the Ad Exchange and DSP. DSP then determines the key characteristics of the impression like demographic information, browsing history, location, and the page being loaded and tries to analyse if that impression is suitable for the advertiser. If it finds it suitable then it examines how much the advertiser can bid for that and then revert back with its bid value to the SSP through Ad Exchange. SSP receives the bid value from all the advertiser's DSP and then finds out which advertiser is bidding the highest value. As soon as the SSP finds it highest bidder it immediately transfers the ad space to the browser of the user and the ad is served on the publisher's website.

Stepwise process: (Basic)

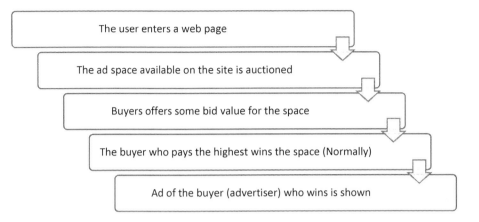

The user enters a web page

The ad space available on the site is auctioned

Buyers offers some bid value for the space

The buyer who pays the highest wins the space (Normally)

Ad of the buyer (advertiser) who wins is shown

Note: The request contains the advertising space and the associated user profile with a unique user ID.

Three major players in RTB are:

1. Demand Side Platform
2. Supply Side Platform
3. Data Management Platform

RTB can be considered as set of rules which helps in evaluating single ad impressions in real time where DSP and SSP is intended to help in the process flow plus adding data from DMP doubles the value of process with the increase in the accuracy of the decision taken.

*We will discuss all the three players in our coming chapters.

Advantages:

- Bid for only what you need:
  RTB enables advertisers to place bids only on those inventory which is best for their campaign. This results in minimizing the wastage of media spend on those impressions which aren't targeting the desired audience. Moreover through RTB, impressions are bought on an individual basis which means paying only for the impression which is relevant for the campaign.

- Publishers can reach out to more advertisers:
  Ad Exchanges in RTB enables publishers to reach out to lot more advertisers. This ensures that publishers make most of their inventory by selling it to the highest bidder.

- Reduced Pricing of Inventory:
  Through RTB, the pricing of the impressions is determined by supply and demand. So, now there isn't any requirement of manual pricing negotiation between the publisher and advertiser. Reduced pricing and better targeting lead to better results for advertisers.

- Publishers work on current market value:
  RTB allows website owners to sell their advertising inventory on a current market value and they be updated about the current rates that are flowing in the market.

- Feasibility on changing campaign setting basis insights:
  RTB software allows advertisers to test and learn easily, exploring how reach and availability fluctuate based on bid price and frequency cap. The real time insight on the campaign helps to take proper practical steps for a successful campaign execution.

- Relevant targeting:
  Addressing relevant users make the advertiser use the budget optimally. RTB allows advertisers to access the inventory that they want to target.

Risks of RTB:

- Declining of price due to increase in supply then demand
- Due to wrong information transmission which is a rare case but if that happens it will lead to increased expenditure for advertiser. The other reason could be due to low presence of data on user profiles after which the technology targets on statistical or probability calculation which may not be always accurate.
- Increased data protection as the leak of data may lead to loss of consumer in many means

Conclusion:

- Website owners have the opportunity to best utilize their existing inventory
- Advertisers are happy due to targeting the apt user profiles at a fair market price
- Wastage of advertising is reduced
- Effectiveness of performance-oriented campaigns has increased at a good rate which was difficult optimizing while doing via affiliate or direct vendors.
- Possibilities of increased targeting
- Advertiser and publisher, both are happy with RTB technology which clearly shows it will play an important role in coming future

DATA MANAGEMENT PLATFROM (DMP)

General Definition of DMP (Data Management Platform):

A centralized system to collect proprietary data, integrate with third-party data and applying that data to an advertising strategy. An advanced data management platform allows users to create custom segments, predict segment volumes, synchronize the segments with other sources, to overlay advanced analytics and is often integrated into DSP platforms or a part thereof.

Simple Definition of DMP (Data Management Platform):

A platform where data's are saved and managed which later on is used to predict purchase intent, make comparisons and majorly on advertising strategy. The platform allows a company to host a single point of all behavioral, business and advertising data in order to analyse issues based on business-as personalization of offers and customer satisfaction.

Technical Definition of DMP
(Data Management Platform):

DMP (Data-Management Platform) data management platform, is the dispersion of the first and third-party data integration into a unified technology platform where then data standardization and segmentation is done so that users can put these results to the current subdivision.

Scenarios with or without DMP (Data Management Platform):

- Before DMP or when data's were not saved:
    o You can probably put ads served to a group of people
    o May cause delays, but still costing
    o Unable to track people willing to buy
- After- new data collection techniques were later applied:
    o Through the record, you know the user's exact preferences
    o Precision lock single user investment and advertising
    o You can track user purchase intention to continue lure them

DMP (Data Management Platform) Working:

DMP consist of three phases:

- Aggregate phase – In this phase data is collected from multiple sources like first party i.e. website, third party, offline data, transaction data, etc. To collect these data placing a tag on the site is the first step
- Integrate and Manage phase – After the data collection, its integration and management are done. Basically, this phase is divided into four stages
    o Storage/warehousing: In this stage only the storage process is done
    o Normalization: Data identification between own and third party is done, all the data refining process is done at this stage (all the data collected are not necessarily important and useful)
    o Selection/Segmentation: The division or segmentation of data is done as per specific rule or common parameter in this stage
    o Analysis and Decision: Complete analysis of the data is done thereafter the evaluation of data is done at this stage

- Deploy phase – In this phase deployment can be done using the data. Reaching to this phase means data is now transferred to information which can be used to form advertising strategy, or business strategy or in any decision making.

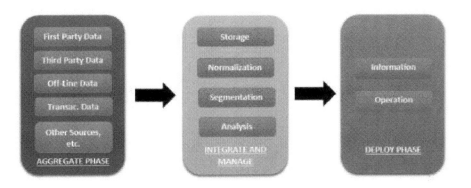

DMP's core elements include:

- Data integration and standardization capability: The unified approach, the parties to absorb data integration.
- Data management capabilities breakdown: To create unique and meaningful customer segments, effective marketing campaigns.
- Functioning data labels: Data labels provide the flexibility, ease of use of marketing activities.
- Self-service user interface: Direct access to web-based data tools integrated web interface or other programs, functions, and several forms of reporting and analysis.
- Relevant channels connected environments: Integration with relevant sources, including websites end, display advertising, e-mail and search and video, allowing marketers to find, locate and deliver highly relevant sub-groups of marketing information.

What are the specific duties of DMP (Data Management Platform)?

DMP is a series of one-stop multi-media advertising platform, and its responsibilities include:

- RECORD DATA:
    o Traffic Sources
    o Cookie
    o FB Id
    o Operation Record

- SAVE DATA:
    o All the data collected are segmented and saved for analysis

- ANALYSE DATA:
    o Analysis, sorting out the visual information chart with statistics

- IDENTIFY TARGET:
    o Mining goal
    o Finishing population
    o Management portfolio
    o Provides objective
    o Provide a target for DSP

After obtaining screening target analysis, it will continue the following processes: Customized ad delivery - Due to advances in technology, and now you can lock a single user to vote customized ads, advertising better than natural. CRM Customer Relationship Management - This is actually a concept of customer management, order conversion cycle to master and user habits, and then formulates advertising strategies. The end result is: *To enhance the accuracy of advertising!*

Types of DMP (Data Management Platform):

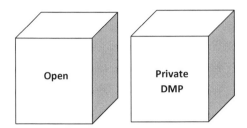

1. Open DMP - Open DMP consists of data related to website visitors, demographic data, interests, audience data, advertising related access data, etc. Advertisers (operating companies or agencies are given access to this DMP)
2. Private DMP - In addition to the area of open DMP, aggregates the proprietary of marketing data such as purchase information, user profiles, various promotion results, etc.

Five main features of DMP:

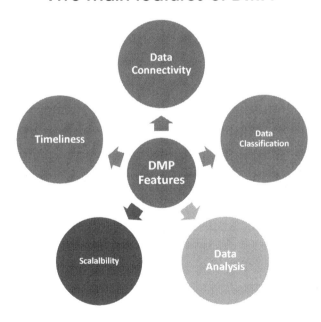

- Data Connectivity: Very important feature of DMP which makes it a master house of data. It has technique to import data from different devices and when required can export the same or blended data to other delivery systems like ad networks, ad exchanges, DSPs or other third parties.

- Data Classification: DMP does not stops at just collecting the data but yes segmenting it properly and converting the data into information, it helps in creating specific unique audience profiles
- Data Analysis: After collecting and classifying, the DMP analyse the same to carve out the user or customer intent or behavior
- Scalability: DMP's one of the core feature is its fluent process to handle huge amount of data and process it perfectly to carve out proper information which can be used to increase the performance of a campaign. Meanwhile the DMP is extracting data from different sources it also simultaneously analyse them on the other hand.
- Timeliness: Very important feature of DMP is its timeliness. It provides data in less than 100 MS to match the typical duration of an auction.

DMP (Data Management Platform) Issues:

- Lot of data maintenance
- Security and privacy concerns
- Considerable amount of cost and time spent during implementation

DMP (Data Management Platform) Advantages:

DMP has main 6 major advantages over manual data management, let's know them all –

1. Data Integration is possible
2. Scalability (Supports the processing of large amounts of information)
3. Speed & Accuracy (It can be processed at high speed with the use of cloud)
4. Flexibility (It can be designed to suit a particular purpose by the platform)
5. Analysis & Discovery is easy to do
6. Robustness (Provides secure platform)

DMP for Marketer vs DMP for Publisher:

When classified by the difference of the user of the DMP, it can be divided into two:

1. DMP for Marketer – It is a case of using the DMP for the purpose of marketing their products and services
2. DMP for Publisher – Here it is used with the purpose of raising advertising value by showing ads to relevant users or database of his site. E.g. to improve the efficiency of advertising by changing the message of the advertisement from the user's profile i.e. different for male and female.

Some of the DMP's in the market:

- LiveRamp
- Acxiom
- Neustar
- DataLogix
- TRA
- Polk
- Blukai
- Bizo

INTRODUCTION TO DSP, SSP AND AD EXCHANGES

DSP - Demand Side Platform:

Definition:

A demand-side platform concept originated in Europe, is a platform which act as a service for advertisers and their agencies. They allow a central platform to efficiently buy inventory through various supply channels (ad networks, ad exchanges and SSPs). Demand side platforms facilitate buyers with direct Real Time Bidding access across multiple sources of inventory. DSPs are directed at advertisers. It enables the buyers to get access to more publishers and then choose the best as per their requirement.

DSPs position themselves both as a pure *technological self-service platform*. Here campaigns by the advertiser / agency is self-created and controlled. To use the DSP as a service, a year contract is concluded usually where the advertiser agrees to pay a minimum monthly commission which could vary between 10 to 20% of the budget. Self Service solutions allow advertisers more direct control, right from bidding to targeting, however, the tools are slightly complex and may require experienced support to achieve best results.

Earlier the common practice in advertising involved digital ads being bought and sold by human ad buyers and salespeople, which were costly and unreliable. DSPs made the process cheaper and more efficient by making it automated and reduced the needs of human intervention. Even there wasn't need of negotiation of ad rates as the process became automated.

DSPs enables advertisers to purchase impressions across a range of publisher site, but targeted to specific users based on information such as their location and their previous browsing behavior.

Now, there has to be a medium through which ad impressions from publishers could be made available to the buyers. Here comes the role of Ad Exchange. Publishers make their ad impressions available through marketplaces called ad exchanges and then DSPs automatically decides which of those impressions would be best suited for the advertiser to buy.

The price of each impression gets decided through real-time auction, a process also known real time bidding. This means there's no need for the salesperson to manually negotiate prices with buyers because the impressions get simply auctioned off to the highest bidder.

Three main roles of a DSP:

1. It assists in technical connection to the supply channels via RTB protocol
2. Allows running in the background for optimization of algorithms for the maximum efficiency of campaigns. The brain of the algorithm lies in the Bidding rules and strategies.
3. DSPs can integrate data from third-party vendors to upgrade which then helps in evaluating the user profiles offered by supply channel for better evaluation of the advertising space

Pros and Cons:

Pros:

- Integrated Platform: DSP provides a comprehensive platform for advertisers and they can manage multiple sources of traffic channels through a single platform, avoiding the waste of resources caused by complex media buying patterns.
- Saves operational cost: As DSP provides one platform for all channels, it avoids extra resources for all different channels.
- Very efficient and targeted
- Transparency: It is one of the key benefits that DSP provides

- Extensive reach: By using DSP advertiser can reach to maximum users with the same targeting that advertiser is intended to apply.
- Simplifies the process of media buying
- Real Time: DSP allows buyers to show a single ad for real-time bidding
- Self-optimization basis the campaign goal set by Advertiser
- Reporting: DSP provides comprehensive reporting, almost all the possible metrics can be included in the report

Cons:

- Very time-consuming and demanding regarding campaigns setup and bidding rules.
- Managed Service Solutions are partially transparent.

Difference between DSP and RTB:

S. No.	Demand Side Platform (DSP)	Real Time Bidding (RTB)
1.	It's a platform that advertisers uses to buy inventory	It's a mechanism by which inventory is bought
2.	Helps to give access to multiple RTB exchanges through one interface	Helps to bid each impression
3.	Helps to buy audiences (collected from behavioral data, cookies, and data exchanges) rather than specific websites	Bid as per the audience selected, website can be any
4.	DSP is an interface for advertisers whereas SSP is an interface for publishers	RTB can be considered as middleware for DSP and SSP
5.	DSP enables global ad frequency capping across exchanges which improve campaign efficiency and user experience.	RTB functions as per the command passed through the DSP that an advertiser is using

Difference between DSP and Ad Network:

S No.	Ad Network	Demand Side Platform (DSP)
1.	It's an online platform which aggregates publisher's inventory	DSP is a platform which helps in bidding on behalf of advertisers
2.	It consists of multiple website and blogs	It consists of multiple ad networks and ad exchanges
3.	The bidding strategy is not real time	The bidding strategy works on real time
4.	Works on multiple pricing models like CPM, CPC, CPE, etc.	Only CPM
5.	The cooperation with DMP is not sure shot and is improper	The cooperation with DMP is kind of mandate as DSP majorly helps in audience targeting which is dependent on data
6.	The inventory is less with respect to DSP	Huge inventory as multiple ad networks with their collection of sites are empanelled

Which DSP can be considered as perfect DSP?

A perfect DSP is the one which has all the below qualities and possibilities:

- Have its own technology including bidders and data centre
- Customization and integration should be possible, especially when adding a tag for data recording.
- Provides end-to-end self-serve interface with support 24x7
- DSP is a technological platform, if not 24x7 but yes most important, technical support should be of high quality
- When required it should also offer managed services
- Multiple Interface language options
- Impressions/Clicks provided should be by country wise and not all over i.e. market liquidity per country is important
- Automatic optimization is recommended, including self-creative optimization
- It should have retargeting capabilities

- Targeting capabilities should be updated, e.g. Geo-targeting should reach till city or pin code and not just country or states
- Real time targeting possibilities
- Quality exchanges covering display, mobile, and video should be well synced
- Auto warning messages should be provided to the trader
- Brand safety should always be self-considered
- Pricing transparency should be there, even if the DSP is charging basis the net cost spent or also basis the trading commission charges, it should be notified beforehand.
- It should not support or be inclined to any specific publisher, exchange, data provider or any vendor.
- Timely auto billing
- Presence of billing in local currency is a big advantage
- Etc., these are the basics that a DSP should have, above this adds on to its quality and potentiality.

SSP - Supply Side Platform:

Definition:

A supply-side platform is the publisher's equivalent of a DSP. Where DSPs are used by marketers to buy ad impressions from exchanges as cheaply and as efficiently as possible, SSPs are designed by publishers to do the opposite i.e. to maximize the prices of their impressions that they sell. It's the similar technology that powers both SSPs and DSPs. It is considered to be a space manager or space optimizer which helps publishers to better manage their inventory and costs and are adopted by publishers because they contribute to their own audience data and protect the brand reputation. The true fact of SSP is that it currently represents the largest online display inventory.

It allows publishers to connect their inventory to multiple ad exchanges, DSPs, and networks at once. This, in turn, allows a huge range of potential buyers to purchase ad space and for publishers to get the highest possible rates. When an SSP throws impressions into ad exchanges, DSPs analyse and purchase them on behalf of marketers depending on certain attributes such as where they're served, and which specific users they're being served to. The idea is that by opening up impressions to as many potential buyers as possible — often through real-time auctions — publishers can maximize the revenues they receive for their inventory.

On the SSP service platform, the media can not only own stock inventory in real-time display, but can also work with Ad Exchange, DSP and other digital marketing modules for docking, instant sale, or get to show revenue optimization. SSP has made the selling of inventory very convenient and is actually a boon to publishers. All the technology like SSP, DSP, Ad Exchange, and DMP can be seen as future trends and simultaneously their collaboration can be seen as successful future in the digital industry.

Relation between SSP and DSP:

Now we very well know what SSP is and what DSP is, let's get the insight of their connection with each other and how do they help to serve a potential ad keeping both publisher and advertiser happy.

SSP and DSP makes a closed loop where the intermediate between the two remains the RTB technology, this interworking between the two happens in two ways —

1. Intermediation, and
2. Direct Access

Intermediation:

In this process, both SSP and DSP accesses an ad exchange from where the DSP buys an ad slot whereas SSP sells it. To simplify, when user visits a web page which has an ad slot, the SSP sends a signal with the information like ad slot, user information, etc. to ad exchange for the ad request, the SSP specific ad slot information will be analysed by matching the user attribute information from DMP, after which the package is sent to each DSP and DSP begins to show ads on this bid, the winning bid advertisers makes the way out and his ad is shown on the specific ad slot, thereby allowing the terminal users see. Simultaneously, the other side DSP is connected to ad exchange which sends a signal to exchange to run the ad, after which the information is analysed and right ad slot is picked to show the ad. The process is called intermediation due to the presence of ad exchange which connects both the platform.

Direct Access:

In some marketing services platform, SSP bypasses Ad Exchange and exchange directly with DSP resources. This process does not involve a lot of analysis which was managed by ad exchange in intermediation process but is slight quick in taking the decision to fill the ad slot.

Advantages:

- Targeting becomes possible for each impression
- Improves media revenues
- Helps in fluent media management
- Management of remnant inventory is very well taken care by SSP, which also helps in making high revenue out of it.

SSP Self-Optimization:

Now we all know how online advertising has grown immensely and is still growing which is also raising concern in managing everything perfectly. SSP being the seller platform for the publisher has a goal of maximizing the benefit of each, meanwhile managing the quality traffic to DSP or advertisers. SSP by a platform is itself quite smart and evaluate each impression being sold. By the help of data integration and relevant segments SSP optimize the media and takes the proper decision, they always do a pre optimal screening with respect to many aspects like geography, quality, profile, etc. in order to maximize the value of the flow plus maintaining the brand safety which almost all SSP assures of it.

These all steps are done in Nano seconds while maintaining the quality. Not every SSP may be fully accurate but yes the one with super optimization technology assures to be transparent and sells quality traffic while maintaining the revenue of publishers.

SSP platform also provides complete, comprehensive and multi-dimensional reports for the media which helps in taking better marketing decisions. These reports become an additional source of optimization as basis the reports some manual steps are taken helping vendors take out the best of the platform.

Advantages of SSP:

- Helps publishers earn more money for their inventories by getting better rates whereas SSP also avoids having vacant space or unsold inventory which helps publisher utilize each impression to earn money
- Makes the selling process much easier and efficient
- Avoids manual intervention of sales guy to each advertiser for business, which helps both publisher and advertiser to save time
- Helps in cracking private deals with various advertisers
- Customized auction setup and pricing strategies: Manage all constellations and contractual matters in one user interface. Whether open auctions, fixed placement, guaranteed inventory or deal IDs, the publisher specifies its pricing strategies and the rules for offering its inventory to the buy side – across all advertising channels.
- SSP provides detailed live reporting which helps evaluate the media deliveries
- The word SSP has made a lot of buzz in the industry but the true fact is that it's very easy to handle and user-friendly platform.

Ad Exchange:

Definition:

An ad exchange is a digital marketplace that enables advertisers and publishers to buy and sell advertising space, often through real-time auctions. They're most often used to sell display, video and mobile ad inventory.

Simply, an ad exchange is a big pool of ad impressions. It's a platform where publishers put their ad impressions into the pool hoping someone will buy them. Buyers then pick which impressions they wish to purchase using technologies like demand-side platforms. Those decisions are often made in real time based on information such as the previous behavior of the user an ad is being served to, time of day, device type, ad position and more. It is considered to be the most emerging way of selling and buying of ads on the internet.

Few major Ad Exchanges includes Right Media which is owned by Yahoo and DoubleClick Ad Exchange which is owned by DoubleClick.

Why did ad exchange come into existence?

The major reasons for the emergence of an ad exchange were due to the heavy uplift in the online advertising market. Every next day the advertising market was growing for some percentage. As more and more ad networks were on the market, the method of delivery of advertising was becoming increasingly complex and less transparent which was raising a concern to advertisers. There was a time when there were more offers than demand, the market was quite haphazard with increased commissions for each ad network, increased time intervals to a sale of advertising space and increased complexity of the sales process. Hence ad exchange came into picture bundling various ad networks creating a single point for advertisers and publishers. It used the same technology that google use for search ads i.e. Real time bidding which enabled the pricing for the publisher optimized (yield optimization) and to access the Advertiser to various providers of advertising space.

Reason with respect to advertiser and publisher:

Advertiser	Publisher
Advertiser was spending too much time and effort in concluding from where to buy the ad spaces in less cost and of course with performance as expected	Publisher was spending too much time and effort in allocation of inventory plus in calculation to carve out the best revenue out of the same

Ad Exchange working when dealing with Ad networks:

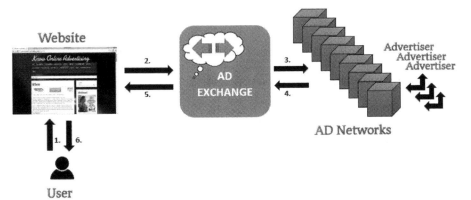

Step 1.

User visits a web page say www.knowonlineadvertising.com, where there is an ad slot available which is being sold via an ad exchange

Step 2.

Web page then makes a request to the linked ad exchange sharing below information:

- Minimum price or bid for the ad space plus the ad dimension required
- User information, whatever the website holds for the same user (based on cookies). Website may or may not pass the user information so in many case exchange can also analyse the user depending on which the ad is shown

Note: It is assumed that the exchange knows the website content plus the ad slots available, depending on which exchange fills the ad slot so there could be cases when ad slot information is not shared – Completely depends on the algorithm.

Step 3.

Ad exchanges are linked with many ad networks to which exchange requests for an ad basis the below information shared:

- Website information which consists of category, keywords, ad slots, etc.
- User information, this information may not be the same as website shared but mix of both website and exchange had the information about the same user
- Price information

Note: There could be scenario when website does not want ad exchange to disclose the real identity of the site so in that case ad exchange can share the relevant information to the ad networks but not real identity

Step 4.

After the request made to different ad networks, all the ad networks response back on behalf of multiple advertisers that they are aligned with. The response includes the below information:

- The maximum price that they are willing to pay for the ad slot,
- The ad that they are willing to show on the same ad slot

Note: The ad network may also choose not to response back with any bid. It's not mandatory for them to reply back.

Step 5.

Once the ad exchange receives the response from multiple ad networks, it runs its algorithm to choose the winning bid or the ad to be shown on the website that made the request. Once the winner is chosen by the ad exchange, the winning network gets to know the outcome and prepares to serve the ad. Also, all the losing networks get the response back of their not winning the bid. The ad exchange algorithm not only plays on the bid but also the ad that has been returned by the networks as it should also match to the website whereas the user too.

Step 6.

The website serves the ad on its slot which is then shown to the user. This is called an impression which is counted on the ad network, publisher Ad server plus also in the ad exchange so that the discrepancy does not come at the end while reporting

All the above processes are done in Nano seconds due to which the user never face any delay in viewing the ad. Ad exchange response rate is very important for all the verticals aligned to it.

Ad Exchange as a "Solution Provider"

With the existence of an ad exchange many problems were solved by bringing solutions in multiple ways:

- It provided a single interface or point of contact between the advertisers and publishers, making it simpler and easy to handle the online buying selling business
- Ad exchange helped the advertisers to buy and compare the ad spaces available, much more convenient to analyse and decide on the same. It also made it convenient for advertisers to modify their buying strategy basis the performance in real time

- The publisher got the solution with respect to inventory allocation whereas also a boost in maximizing the revenue.
- Almost negligible chance of under delivery with the campaign as the buying and selling is done basis the availability and not forecasting keeping both advertiser and publisher happy

Who can participate in an Ad Exchange?

Not any publisher can participate in an ad exchange but has to fulfil many requirements to get sign up. It's the same way as stock exchange works where only large brokerage houses get the entry, so the bigger publisher plus ad networks or ad agencies can apply.

Some of the conditions w.r.t to Google Ad Exchanges are:

- Large volume, almost over 10,000,000 ad impressions
- Generates high CPC
- AdSense approved site gets the access quickly than the ones does not have
- Website with quality content and traffic both. If the source of traffic is organic than the changes go higher to get approved
- Website already signed up with DFP and running ads via the same
- History of running more of banner ads than text ads

There could be some more but if all the above is valid, the publisher can certainly apply.

NOTE: It's not important for the advertiser or publisher both to have their own account in ad exchange to make benefit out of it but we can always use third party like AdWords for advertiser whereas ad sense for publishers. Yes, we can't keep the level same for direct and indirect access but yes the possibility is still there if you don't have direct access.

How does an ad exchange make money?

A lot of people has this question in their mind and have multiple reasons for ad exchange revenue model, some have it right and some not. So let's talk about all the correct options on which ad exchange revenue model works so that the confusion goes away!

- First and foremost is the setup Fee that they charge; this can be a flat rate.
- As a publisher you pay the commission out of the budget spent by the advertiser on the website, the percentage may reach to 20% also. E.g. if 5% is the commission then the inventory bought of $10,000 will make him pay $500 to the exchange he is making use of. Some exchanges make the commission out of the requests made to the exchange, i.e. they may have slab as per the number of requests. Just like an ad server charges as per impression slabs.
- As an advertiser also you pay commission to the exchange, the percentage depends on the exchange plus the deal between the both.

The above three are the major reasons by which ad exchange makes money, just the deals may vary accordingly!

Difference between Ad Exchange and Ad Network:

S.No.	AD EXCHANGE	AD NETWORK
1.	Auction based selling or buying. It helps driving up the value of each ad space as bidding is done on each and every ad impression	Bulk buying of impressions and not auction methodology for each ad impression which is done via ad exchange. Ad networks generally buy bulk impressions from different publishers at lower eCPM
2.	Open Network	Private Network
3.	Transparency level is high in ad exchanges as advertiser or agency have visibility on the site, ad unit and audience that they are bidding on.	Ad network is generally blind network where advertiser just gets the performance report but are not aware where the campaign is running, on request some top performing sites you may get to know but not the complete inventory
4.	Transparency level for publishers are also high as they are clearly aware of which advertisers are bidding on their ad spaces	Whereas publishers are unaware of advertiser information, they can only get to know by looking at the site in a live environment.
5.	As the advertiser buys the ad inventory in real time, they can anytime allocate or reallocate budget depending on the performance	Here the inventory is bought in bulk and cannot change instantly due to poor performance or due to any reason.

6.	Publisher's operational effort is saved via ad exchanges as the buying is done as per availability, so the scare of under delivery or over delivery is very much minimal	Though the inventories are sold as per future forecasting, under delivery is always a chance
7.	Publishers can always set floor price for their ad spaces	Very rare ad networks work on floor prices conditions
8.	Category of inventory is premium, non-premium and even remnant but low inventory as generally sold in low cost and not as same rate via ad networks	Category of inventory is very non-premium/remnant inventory
9.	Pricing is based on real time bidding i.e. as per demand	Pricing is negotiable based on inventory availability
10.	Ad exchanges are famous for its varieties of inventory availability	Ad networks may not have varieties but specificity

Trading Desk:

An entity or organisation which helps advertisers or agency in audience buying.

- It is layered on top of DSP and other audience buying technologies.
- It is a platform that uses data and technology to help advertisers purchase ad inventory and audience more effectively and in real time.
- With the advent of new technologies and targeting tools, the process of buying audience became more transparent and automated.
- In short, it's an audience buying company

It is basically is an internal purchasing platforms agencies for display, Mobile, and video inventory.

In reality, the concept comes from the financial world, where a Trading Desk is an operating table where all investors feel to make purchases in real time. Leaving in question the definitions and results can contribute to an open conception.

Why Agency Trading Desk did came into existence?

High Operational Cost:

In managing media campaigns it generally requires too much of operational work which then calls for more operational people who can help manage campaigns and that requires more investment. Due to the increasing operational cost a lesser investment option was required, ATD becomes that replacement as it saves a lot of operational work and can be self-managed on one interface.

The need of In House Platform:

The need of agency having its own platform where they can buy inventory directly for clients. This brings transparency and trust of the client towards the agency.

The inclination towards the audience buying: As advertising technology has grown, media has moved more towards buying of the audience rather than placements on websites. Now this move has brought a bigger impact on the industry plus doubles the efforts, moving on or having its own trading desk eases in the process of buying basis the audience.

Reduction of waste impressions:

There has been always a discussion and requirement to reduce the waste of impressions by serving only to the potential user. There had been chances when 60-70% of impressions are served to users who are not at all interested in the advertiser's product and to reduce this a proper buying of the audience is required which ATD helps to achieve, saving money indirectly also.

High competition:

With the growth of programmatic buying there is also a growth in the competition which calls for some extraordinary effort to keep you out of the crowd. We all know trading desk controls the programmatic buying very efficiently while maintaining the transparency so agency having its own trading desk flags a trust and attraction towards the clients. It's basically an add-on in winning new clients.

Increasing Client's demand towards ownership or control:

Today clients are well educated about the online industry and want to be aware of very activity that agency is taking for their campaign. They demand of more insight and control of the campaign i.e. majorly the transparency which calls for a need of trading desk as trading desk gives ownership and control to the client if required, both in respect of data and campaign that is live.

Benefits of Trading Desk:

- Improved Targeting:
  Trading desk helps to target audience on one to one basis by matching certain criteria. They prepare the list of criteria that defines audience behavior and then with the use of DSP it matches inventory and audience attribute which optimizes campaign performance. On a fact, there is no platform or technology which can assure 100% accuracy in targeting but yes trading desk does boast a nearly as good value. It helps in tracking user behavior and creates a blended audience list which can be targeted accordingly to the campaign brief or targeting requirement. If in case the target selected is not apt, we can always change the targeting in real time which can save or help in minimizing the unwanted impressions.

- Improves Campaign Performance:
  Trading desk performs detailed data analysis which helps in knowing how the campaign is performing and what are the shortcomings.

- Increased ROI:
  Agency trading desk primarily goal is to increase the profit margin i.e. the ROI and this is well achieved using ATD.

- Saves operational cost:
  Operational cost smoothly goes down as the trading desk is well furnished to be managed by less number of people. This brings one more big reason for an agency to have its own trading desk

- Advertising Effectiveness:
  It increases day by day as testing of various platforms is a common practice which can be easily done is a very minimal cost.

- Reliable Service:
  Agency trading desks are not based on third-party networks or provider which allows you to rely on their services and are better integrated. Due to the trading desk, an agency has direct control over the expenditure on the target group and is able to provide more input to make the most out of the client budget. This brings more reliability and confidence of the client towards the agency to spend more budget.

- Extensive Data Analysis:
  At the end of the campaign or even in the middle of it, trading desk can provide clients with comprehensive analysis which ensures the client about right targeting. The same data helps in enhancing the campaign performance which assures in achieving the campaign goal bringing better ROI at the end.

- Stimulates budget towards digital:
  Trading desk has quite increased the trust of clients towards the digital advertising which eventually force them to spend more budget on digital, there has been number of time when the money has been carved out of offline bucket to spend on digital which clearly shows the spend on digital has increased and is expected to grow more and more.

Where do we see the trading desk in Programmatic buying ecosystem?

Major Trading Desks:

Trading Desk	Agency Group
Amnet	Aegis
Accuen	Omnicom Group
Cadreon	IPG
Vivaki	Publicis
Xaxis	WPP
Adnetik	Havas

MALVERTISING

Definition:

Malvertising refers to cyber-criminal attacks which use online advertising channels to infiltrate malicious code and malware into the user's computers. Accessing these codes can harm user's computer even to the extent of damaging the data files or stealing personal information.

Working:

There are different ways by which attackers can spread Malware. The malicious code can be placed in the ad itself thus making the ad infected or clicking the ad could redirect the users to the site which is infected with malware. Usually, what advertiser does is, in the beginning they serve clean ads which do not contain malware and once they start getting the major traffic they put a malicious code behind those ads, accessing which harms the visitor's computer with malware.

Publishers, who accept the ads directly from the advertisers and publish them on their sites, need to be very careful. If they publish an infected ad it's a risk for their site visitors and also for their own reputation. So, once an ad is accepted, the publisher should run some checks and scans to make sure that the ad is infection free.

Generally, when the ads are submitted to the network, they go through the scans to ensure that they are clean and not contain any infected code. But, these scans can never be perfect.

For e.g. accessing lot of sites shows pop up ads on it, showing attractive offers or saying that you have won prize money. Most of those are the attempt by advertisers to spread malware.

Online Trust Alliance:

OTA (online trust alliance) provides some guidelines which can be followed by both publishers and advertisers to evaluate the integrity of the data used in the advertisement. This evaluation can help in protecting the users from accessing the infected data.

Below are few guidelines provided by OTA, following these can be of great help in preventing against malware attacks:

- Ad Serving Domain Risk Factors:
  - o How long it's been registered?
  - o How active is the domain?
  - o Has the domain been recently transferred to or from a 3rd party?
- Ad Tag Risk Factors:
  - o Does the tag use flash code?
  - o Does clicking on tag gives warning message?
- Corporate /Website Risk Factors:
  - o How does the site look? Should it not look unprofessional?
  - o Does the site have obvious errors?
  - o Does the site has legal SSL Certificate and Expiration of Certificate?
- Individual Risk Factors:
  - o Check for the identity of the contact.
  - o Does the email address correspond to corporate site?
  - o Does the reply email address bounce?
- Reputation:
  - o Check their reputation with other well-known and trusted service provider.
  - o How stable are they when it comes to working with a service provider. Do they frequently change service providers and ad servers?

Types of Malware attacks:

- Banners with malicious code.
- Third party ads and applications on the web page.
- Pop-Up ads.
- Hidden iframes on the web page.

Some Preventive Measures:

- Don't blindly trust the advertiser.
- Check for the reputation of the advertiser in the market.
- Use latest versions of browsers and software which could have additional security features. E.g. Use the latest version of Internet Explorer.
- Use anti-virus software capable enough of trapping malicious codes.

AD BLOCKING

What is Ad blocking?

Ad blocking is no technology but just about blocking of ads by the user if he/she is not interested to see any ad when he or she visits any website. To understand ad blocking functionality let's know the product called adblock plus which helps user block ads for them.

Interestingly Ad blockers can also go at a level of hardware and can block the ads at router level. It can plug into the internet router and can help blocking ads for all the IP's passing via the same. This method is generally used by companies who wants to block ads and want to apply the filter at a company level. E.g. AdTrap

What is AdBlock Plus?

AdBlock plus is built using Gecko technology which is a web browser engine developed by Mozilla Foundation. Gecko works on a concept of 'Content Policies' which is a JavaScript or C++ object that is called whenever the browser is requested to load something (e.g. website loading). The content policy is a code which plays a role in allowing what to be loaded and what not, there are multiple content policies with different definitions e.g. it could include no image loading for a site, different content as per browser, etc.

AdBlock has no default functionality and it does not block until unless the user asks for it. AdBlock is a functionality which is completely dependent on filters and these filters are nothing but a set of rules that directs the adblock to work on or basically block that user is not interested to see, like ads on the website. Using these filters you can also block malware, third party tracking's, etc. To lot of it may feel that adding extension to the browser plays the role in blocking but the fact is the extension only gives the direction; it's the same Gecko (web engine) technology which plays the role in blocking. The blocking ads are not that tough to do as it is well known that ads rendered from a different server and not the same from where the content is deployed thus making it easy to identify tags and advertising code in the page which is removed before the call is made to the ad server.

The default filters that are applied for default are:

- An ad-blocking list selected based on your language (EasyList)
- The Acceptable Ads list

NOTE: These default list can also be removed if not interested

Simple Working via image:

Step 1:

A user opens any website on his browser, as soon as the request goes to the servers for content and ad, simultaneously Adblock addon or extension which is installed in your browser comes in action too.

Step 2:

Adblock does all the processing, blocking as per the filters applied

Step 3:

Adblock blocks all the ads to appear on the website and the website is seen as per below image. The ad spot layout can also be changed showing the user as if there was no ad spot available, but for that CSS and condition coding has to be done.

Adding to above three steps, there are multiple processing done, like ad server call, web server call, browser processing, etc. But in the summary below image gives you the idea what action does ad blockers does.

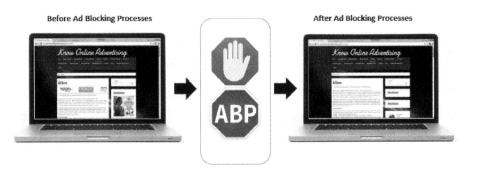

Before Ad Blocking Processes   After Ad Blocking Processes

How Adblock plus blocks ads?

Three main functionality Adblock uses are:

1. Request blocking - This ensures to block the HTTP request which will prevent from loading thus saving in unnecessary requests and responses. This makes the page load faster, it includes:
   o   Blocking of known domain and sub-domain from loading ads e.g. atdmt, ad, etc.
   o   Blocking of servers which associates with advertisements. It could be any CDN, or google creative server or any third party server also
   o   Blocking of known scripts which help in loading ads
   o   Generally, all kind of iframes is checked before rendering on the page as iframe is well known for serving ads
2. Element hiding - This feature works by injecting CSS code in the website which then helps in hiding the elements that are requested to be blocked, using this the ads are completely removed from the page, but will only help to hide ads but not stopping them from loading ads which will take its own time in the first place thus this slows down the loading of page.
3. Creative (Image) Blocking – Adblock just not block as per domain or sub-domain but also as per image dimensions, common IAB ad sizes like 728x90, 300x250, 160x600, 120x600, 468x60, etc. are blocked no matter they are ads are not. This is done as these sizes are generally ad units placed on websites.

CAREER IN ONLINE ADVERTISING

The online advertising industry has grown like anything and there is still left to see much in coming years, the technology has moved a lot, advertisers has started spending much more than before in online industry which is ultimately leading to a lot of money flow and growth of the industry. A lot of jobs got created in different teams in the industry so to be upfront if the industry grows, grows the people aligned to it.

It's the most successful industry blending the careers perfectly and media is always a fun place to work so it's a blend of work and fun. Let's know each and every team who are responsible for growing this industry and see if you can make you place within any of them

Ad Operation:

It's the backend but the key team in Online advertising company, this team does not interact with the client but with the account managers or media team of the same company who manages the client and sends the request for campaign trafficking. The key role of this department is to traffic i.e. create the campaign as per request i.e. IO (Insertion Order – It's the formal deal or agreement signed between the client and the company who is advertising for them).

When you say "Ad Operation" it actually means the same as the team members of this team operates each and every ad before sending it live on the websites.

Key responsibilities:

- Creation of a campaign
- Any changes on existing campaign
- Troubleshooting
- Reporting
- Optimization

Who should join?

The ones with slight technical knowledge and is interested in learning more and more in technical and backend of online advertising should join this department. The team player of this team knows the maximum about the campaign in fact about online advertising as they are the ones who works at the backend i.e. right from the campaign start to end. Ideally starting a career from operation to an account manager or any business team in online advertising makes the person smarter than the crowd.

Account Management:

The name says it all – This team manages the account i.e. client. Not all account managers will service the client but their main role is to furnish the account that they are responsible for. They get the request from clients or client servicing/Sales people which they finally send it to ad operation team to get it executed. This team keeps a check on accounts to see everything is running in flow and the campaign will deliver on time if any glitch they communicate to the client and takes the decision after the discussion.

Accounts managers are assigned to sales people i.e. the sales bring business and account managers process them.

Key responsibilities:

- Managing and furnishing accounts
- Optimization is also their part of role
- Sending request to ad operation team
- They communicate with Sales people
- Communicate with Finance team to get the formal agreement done
- Communicate with creative team to get the creative done

Who should join?

This team is the best fit for MBA guys and the ones who are interested in management stuff rather than technical. A person has to be patient and knows how to get the work done. This role requires a lot of communication with different teams. Slowly with experience, you may require to handle multiple accounts at a time so management powers and setting up right priority is very important

Campaign Management:

This team takes care of multiple campaigns that are running, they decide on the campaign strategy and execution. This team is a mixture of ad operation and account manager, you don't need to traffic a campaign but should have insight understanding about the system as you are key responsible of taking a decision on campaign execution plan.

The team suggests further steps which will help in successful campaign execution, either they send the request to account managers or directly to ad operation team keeping account manager's informed about the steps. They don't communicate with the client but internally in the company.

Key responsibilities:

- Management of multiple campaigns i.e. an account may have 10 campaigns simultaneously
- Analytics and data crunching
- Understanding of campaign reports
- Communication with Ad operation and account management team
- Optimization is a major role as it helps in strategy building

Who should join?

This team is the best fit for the ones who are interested in both management and technical side. It requires an awesome analytics skill as you play more with data, the ones who doesn't like excel and numbers much shouldn't try as basis on the numbers next steps are taken

NOTE: Some companies take Campaign managers as ad operation team, and then their ad operation team takes care of both campaign execution and decision on next steps

Publisher Development:

This team is seen only in networks and not in agencies or publishers. The team takes care of different publishers that are aligned with the system and their responsibility is to help in making the publisher network more i.e. bringing more publishers in the list.

They communicate with different publisher or website owner for ad space or pricing related issues. The agenda of this team is to keep track of publishers and requires not much of internal interactions

Key responsibilities:

- Communication with different publishers
- Check on existing publishers and their bids
- Ad space creation
- Publishers Ad tag creation which is then shared by respective publishers
- Management of multiple publishers, the list could be in 1000's
- Internal communication with the management team

Who should join?

Not necessarily MBA but anyone who knows management and have perfect communication skills can join this team. This team does not require a lot of technical skills whereas knowledge about campaign executions and all so who is interested in being part of online adverting but is interested in staying out of it and helping the company to rise with respect to some external stuff i.e. like bringing premium publishers at lower rate should go ahead with the team. It's not a target oriented team but requires actions to grow.

Creative:

This is the most creative team in online advertising companies as it requires a lot of creativity in building banners for the client. This team creates banners right from designing to development. Not every individual does the same as the team divides between developer and designer, i.e. designers are the one who designs the graphics or the look of the banner whereas developers are the one who codes the banner i.e. it's actions.

Key responsibilities:

- Creation of new banners
- Adaptations of ads
- Creative strategy
- Coding i.e. development
- Communication with Account managers and ad operation team

Who should join?

Of course joining this team requires prior knowledge of flash creation or development. The person who is good in designing or arts can take a step ahead in designing team. Complete technical knowledge about creative is required. No management and no knowledge of online advertising are required.

Sales:

The target oriented team is the sales team, this team complete responsibility is to bring business to the company, the people under this team pitches different clients or agencies to bring some campaigns. It's like the same other sales job and requires understanding of what they are selling

Key responsibilities:

- Pitching clients
- Presentation
- Management of accounts till they are handed to the respective account managers
- Direct communication with the clients
- A lot of travelling i.e. less sitting in office

Who should join?

The ones who love travelling and is very smart in convincing people should go ahead with this team. The ones who think are very confident and can convince in taking their product should surely go to this team as it has bonus bringing more business whereas if you enjoy meeting new people than it's a perfect role for you. MBA's are preferred for this team but if the company is small or start up graduates may get a chance to hit the role

Product/Ad server (Engineering):

If the company has their own ad server this team is the most important as they take care of the successful running of the server which is helping to run the complete business. This team is full of engineers, could be a coder, developer, product managers, database experts, etc. It's a complete technical team who takes care of backend of the whole system.

The team is responsible for the perfect execution of ad server plus enhancement of it.

Key responsibilities:

- Coding or development
- Internal communication with the management
- Release of new code
- Troubleshooting in the server
- Enhancement i.e. new ideas that can make the ad server compatible of taking all kind of requests and doing perfect targeting
- Algorithm writing

Media Planning:

It's one of the key team in advertising agency whose goal is to create a perfect plan out of the budget provided by the client. Their clear agenda is to identify the best possible media who can help maximize the impact of their advertising campaigns. It's one of the fancy team I would say as publishers keep running after them to get on a plan of their next campaign. They work in sync with client servicing or account manager team to understand the business objective, once the plan is live, they work in sync with operation team to get the plan delivered on time.

Key Responsibilities:

- Working with client, account managers, ad operation and also creative agencies
- Decision making on the best medium to advertise on

- Identifying target audiences and analysing their characteristics
- Presenting proposals initially and post evaluation at the end of the campaign to clients
- Meet multiple vendors or publishers to discuss the inventory and data availability
- Work on different tools like comScore and social platforms

Who can join?

The one with good communication skills, factual analysis, creative thinking, and always interested to speak to multiple people as the role requires a lot of communication before the plan gets final. The planner needs to speak to multiple publishers for their media rates and availability. Some agencies have separate media buying team where the rates closure is done by them, the planner just has to close the deal basis strategy and availability.

Media Buying:

The team in an ad agency who is solely responsible for buying media or inventory on different websites. Media buyers negotiate, purchase and monitor the advertising space bought, their agenda is to buy premium spaces at low cost and for best possible rates, they may make a deal with the vendor on a monthly, quarterly or yearly basis. The decision completely remains with them. The team is not generally client specific and works for more than one client simultaneously. Media buyers tend to work alongside media planners when executing media-based promotional strategies for their clients.

Key Responsibilities:

- Networking – Develop relationships with multiple vendors, especially the important ones
- Negotiation is one important task of a media buyer as they have to bring the best possible rate on table
- Tracks media expenditures to ensure agency and client budget compliance.
- Presentation to clients on the media they bring on table at best possible rates
- Assimilate large amounts of information

Who can join?

The person who loves to communicate, have analytical thinking, good at numbers, negotiating attitude, persuasive, plus a good researcher is perfect for this role and simultaneously would enjoy the same. The role is more of similar to a planner role, it's just they don't sit and make excel plan to present to the client but helps the planner in making the same.

Client Servicing:

This team has one important task to handle i.e. clients. They are the ones who faces the clients and note down their requirement or expectation out of a specific campaign or generally with the team even. They can be considered as a bridge between the client and agency. Some agencies have client servicing team who also looks after generating new clients plus retaining the ones already empanelled with the agency. They help in selling the plan made by the planner and so the team should have clear understanding on the plan that is being presented, the team members should have fair knowledge about online advertising industry

Key Responsibilities:

- Generating new clients
- Maintaining and servicing existing clients
- PR
- Furnishing of the brief shared by the client to creative, planning, buying team.
- Brainstorming with the media team on the brief
- Designing new schemes to attract new clients or pursued the same client to spend more.
- Arranging and attending meetings
- Making pitches

Who can join?

Client servicing requires a person with awesome communication skills, confident, manipulative, patient, and excellent presentation skills.

Social Media:

Rising team in the online advertising industry, today all advertiser has realized that presence in the social platform is very important and so is the rise. This team takes care of multiple social platforms including Facebook, Twitter, LinkedIn, etc. where they not only work on paid campaigns but also organic reach. The team creates plan as per the budget and targeting shared by the client or media planners in an advertising agency (depends on the agency has just social account or complete account with them)

Key Responsibilities:

- Planning and goal setting
- Content Management
- Reporting analysis
- Social activity analysis of competitor brands
- Strategy creation
- Work closely with Legal to ensure compliance with company branding and social media disclosure guidelines

Who can join?

If you love the social platform and if you are creative this is the role you fit in. Social platforms are real time and so requires close look on the activity. Content writing is an important part of social advertising so the ones with good hands on in content writing should try this field of online advertising. And the most important is the positive attitude towards life and work both.

Manufactured by Amazon.ca
Bolton, ON